The Life of a
BOWERBIRD

creating beautiful interiors
with the things you collect

SIBELLA COURT

Photography
by Chris Court

HARPER DESIGN

An Imprint of HarperCollins Publishers

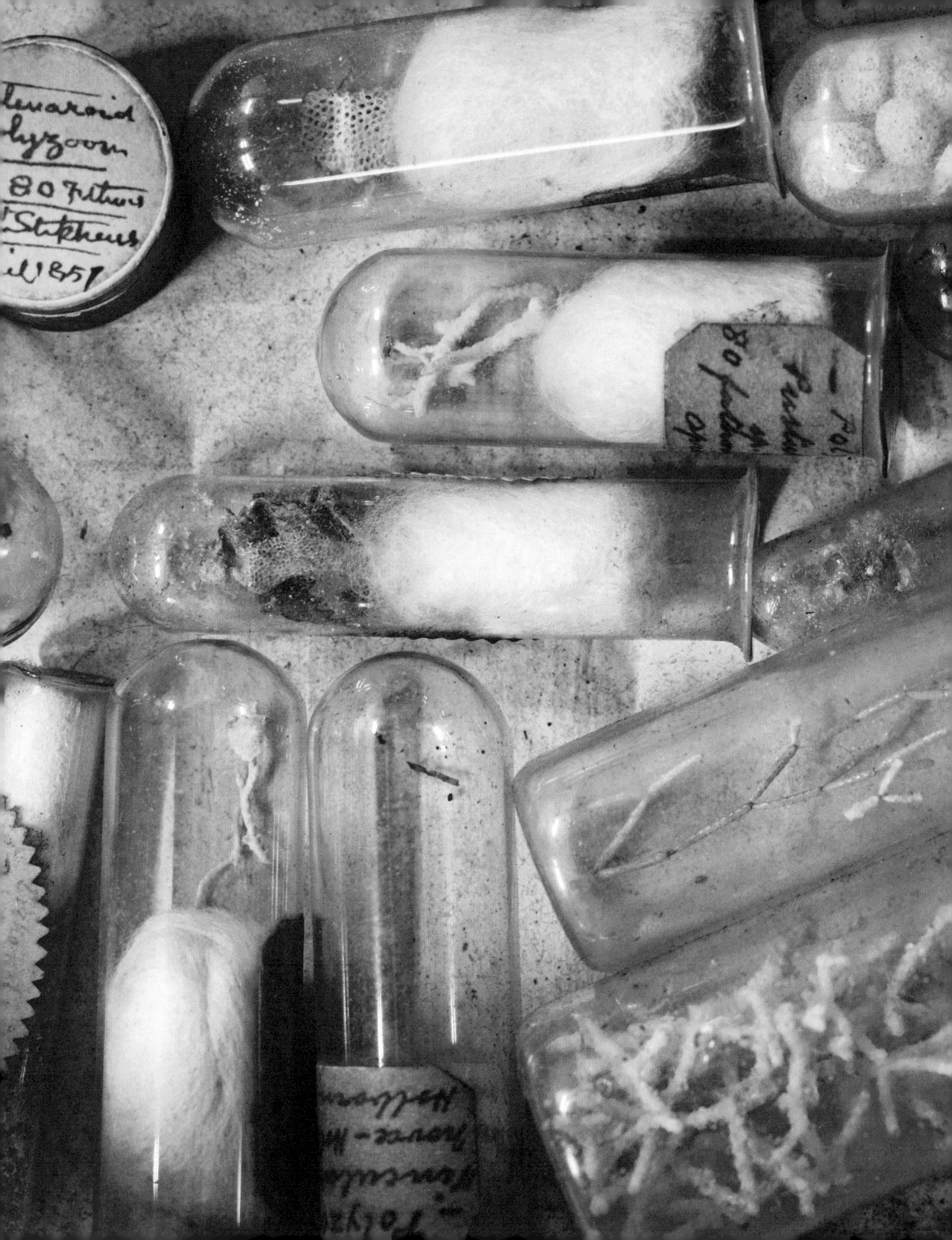

CONTENTS

The biography of a BOWERBIRD

A bowerbird is an Australian native bird that builds a reedy ground nest and goes to extraordinary lengths to decorate it with "stolen" goods and found objects such as shells, bones, pegs, and shiny milk caps. I have been referred to as a bowerbird, and like to think of myself as a finder, keeper, & curator of collections & beautiful things. This is my biography.

My first collections from around the age of three or four (which I still possess) were shells, sequins, beads, and ribbons. They encapsulate my childhood, my mother, our holiday house, early school years, solitary moments, playing with my siblings, and other lovely fleeting thoughts.

All objects, once held, have a memory or story of where, when (sometimes a bit vague), and who you were with when you found them. I have a better memory for such things and none for last week's incidents. I am renowned for my extensive collections and draw on them constantly for inspiration to create paint colors, give my books layers & texture, style shoots, shop displays, and my own home, as inspiration for stationery and graphic design work and the commercial interiors I design. I enjoy having my things around me: out on show and ready for their story to be told; as rotating objects & treasures; available to touch & turn over.

I call it organized chaos. Lucky for me, I have the luxury of having an outlet for such a habit: my shop, The Society inc. It is here that I constantly get asked how to display treasures & finds. Because I have embraced my tendency to collect rather than attempt to control it, people feel like I have said it is OK to collect — now I need to take it to the next step and show you what to do with all your stuff.

At The Society inc. I have slowly replaced all the cheap & nasty hardware with vintage pieces I have collected over the years. These pieces are made with aesthetic vision, consideration, & care: drawer pulls, light switches, window sashes, towel racks, shaving mirrors, and the like. On my desk, I work with all my old-fashioned office paraphernalia: stapler, brown paper holder, staples, docket pin, holepunch, and bulldog clips. On my walls I have mounted & framed shells, entomological finds, and botanical specimens that sit together in natural history harmony. Both upstairs & downstairs there are open floor-to-ceiling shelves, accessed by a Putnam rolling library ladder, so I can see and access all my bits & bobs and global treasures for photo shoots, color boxes, and reference. They are on high rotation between upstairs not-for-sale and downstairs in the shop, depending on whether I feel as though I can part with them on that particular day (most stay upstairs).

What is a collection?
Collect (s); [ing]; -ions-

One or more things. I believe you can start a collection with one thing. Don't be formal – if you like rope, you can start with a braided lanyard with a bottle opener on the bottom. Maybe it's the material that's the collection, although it doesn't need to be the same format – you can put together things made of rope, string, and twine. Or it could be an idea – things that fly, for example. There doesn't have to be any reason for it, a collection doesn't need to be justified beyond the desire to have it and keep it. Collections are simply an attraction (over & over again) to the same object, or shape, or color, or texture.

I have broken this book into ten chapters representing what I love and what sparks my curiosity: Beachcombing; Objet Trouvé; Zoologie/Entomology; Tinctures, Apothecary, & Alchemy; Smiths & Tinkers; Drapers & Mills; Ephemera; Honest & Humble; Oddities & Curiosities; and Magic, Tricks, & Lucky Dips. Each theme is broken into the more detailed and specific collections I own. I will show them sometimes merely for their beauty but also to show how to mix them up and integrate them into the home.

A collection is more often than not emotive, with direct connections between you and the objects in it. A collection is a memento of people, places, past times, and experiences – made up of memories of characters you've encountered, meals, globetrotting adventures, explorations and travels, the details of daily life, time spent with friends, gifts, and a million other things.

Think outside the museum or gallery format of categorizing and systematically formalizing a collection. Your collection can encourage interaction, conversation, and involvement. It can have a sense of humor, be a lifelong project, or exist only for one day. The display of a collection should not be static but change to suit the occasion and place – moving from dinner table to a spot outdoors, become an unexpected feature in an entrance area, a home-warming gesture, or an element of celebration. People have heirlooms, pieces they've bought or found, or things they cannot part with, but are lost as to how to incorporate them into their own home. This book will give you the applications and ideas that transform your collection of whatever it may be into a beautiful focal display or subtle reminder of the things you love.

A brief interpretation of the history of collecting

Amateur collecting became quite the trend in the nineteenth century as science began to compete with religion as a way of understanding the world.

Buccaneers, botanists, & the merely curious brought back from their travels to the New World discoveries as simple as pineapples, skeletons, birds' eggs, shells, and native artifacts to – in the case of real life human beings – the frankly outrageous.

While gentleman-explorers and amateur scientists were working on the edges of official practice, members of the general public were looking with a discerning eye at flora & fauna, and collecting by pressing, pinning, preserving, capturing, skinning, maintaining specimens in books, bottles, jars, boxes, domes, and cases to observe, record, and comment.

The personal collections were not particularly organized (not in any scientific way, at least) but were more a showcase of random objects, totally catering to the owners' desires and interests. These Cabinets of Curiosities, which could be anything from souvenir albums to custom-made pieces of furniture, were simply a place of display where pieces could be easily examined, moved, and cast aside if necessary. A show & tell environment that encouraged visitors, debate, and modern opinion in the Age of Enlightenment and world exploration.

For middle class women in particular, who had the time for rambling & combing the countryside and seashore, the plant-hunting phenomenon (including the Victorian Fern Craze) became a hugely popular and socially favored pastime, allowing them some aesthetic and scientific pursuit otherwise denied. Although it was considered a leisure activity rather than a "career," they did contribute to the advancement of study and understanding of botanical nature through one-of-a-kind handmade mounted illustrated albums most notably of seaweed, algae, fern, and wildflowers.

The roots of many museums lie in the eighteenth & nineteenth centuries, a time when the boundaries between categories of high & low, art & science, education & entertainment were not as clear as they are now. The beginning of the twentieth century saw disciplines becoming specialized and a distinct separation being created between all these things, amateur and professional.

Display

When looking at the illustrated Cabinet of Curiosities of Ferrante Imperato's *Dell'Historia Naturale*, Naples 1599, you can see displayed objects, not restricted to cases or cabinets, but filling all the space, even up to the vaulted ceiling, with a stuffed crocodile, upside down, center stage! Don't be shy about creating 3D adaptations of your cabinets as I do with all my interiors. Let things fly, crawl up walls, lean, or sit on the floor. This is organized chaos.

Remember, the process of collecting, discovering "the find," and interaction is as important as the final display — the story it encapsulates exists as much as the object.

Although I refer to a Cabinet of Curiosities I do not mean to build a cabinet for each of your collections or, in fact, even to display them together. Collections do not have to live together. My mother bought a whittled duck once. Throughout the 1980s she acquired, through gifts and her own doing, about 100 ducks that were displayed all together on a table in our formal living room. This idea is not one I enjoy. So now, with my fear of a room full of ducks, I tend to spread my collections everywhere.

I cling to the idea that your pieces are dynamic, can be moved, lent, touched, and experienced by you, your family, and friends. They can be functional as well as decorative pieces. There is nothing better than being able to utilize them in daily life: meals, workspaces, at home, mantels, and wherever.

I have an interpretation of a "cabinet" at my shop, where one can experience intrigue, wonder, & magic, a place to explore, discover, and find meaning and knowledge.

It is your own personal show & tell, a theater of wisdom, and a keyhole vision into your personality and interests — a 3D self portrait. Reveal tales and memories with your collections through object choices, placement, and the way you display them: there can be communication between those objects. I have taken the idea of display to walls, windows, floors, and ceilings, which incorporates sticking, hanging, placing, lying, flying, and putting under glass.

You are the curator of your collections: edit, be selective, picky, or accommodating. These are your collections & objects that make sense to you and make you happy. Make corners to explore, study, and enjoy — anywhere you like: on windowsills, mantels, and dressing tables. Line things up on a baseboard on the floor, place a length of ribbon or fringe over a doorway, stones in the bottom of a bathtub, or hang textiles on a suspended pole from the ceiling. Do not limit yourself with display and, depending on their format and shape, let the collections speak for themselves. Make the world more beautiful, take care but let go — although I talk about being slapdash, it's more a case of casual abandon. Remember the display of your collection can be changed if you are not totally satisfied — embrace the stylist within and rearrange on a whim.

Museum collections

I encourage you to hunt out any small museums in your local area or while you're on vacations and trips. They're often hidden, sometimes tiny, and occasionally in private houses, often bypassed even by the locals. Put on your super sleuth hat and look for obscure signs (which may be handwritten).

I look for museums that cover botanical & medicinal gardens (living museums), herbariums, zoology, shell or conchology, entomology, natural history, marine and bones, curiosity, history, historic houses, and most things in between. Inspiration comes in unexpected forms — I am often led to something by what a curator might have said, a small note on a plaque, donators' names, or an artist's subject matter. Sometimes the thing you end up discovering was not what you set out for, which is just as exciting.

While researching this book I gained access to the curators, directors, vaults, and storage of the Macleay Museum, H. L. White collection of the Museum of Victoria, Herbarium of NSW, Caroline Simpson Library, Musée de la Chasse et de la Nature, and the Museum of Jurassic Technology. There's more information about them in the "My Library" section at the back of the book.

Hunting&collecting

As a bowerbird, I do get fixated on things and enjoy the focus it brings to shopping expeditions and forages through markets. I have never tired of this, and have a love of early morning *jambon baguettes & cafe au lait* whilst scouring & scrambling the trestle tables and backs of vans at Porte de Vanves or other such markets, finding treasures & pre-loved goods: textiles, porcelain, lampshades, ephemera, tableware, stylist-wares, cutlery, small furniture pieces, and other flotsam & jetsam (the stuff you will find displayed on the grassy strip outside The Society inc., on the corner of Alexander & Stewart Street).

If an object is attractive to me both in aesthetic and in story I will add it without judgment of its origins. I am a random collector with an eye for detail. I do not collect expensive things and I find beauty in the forgotten, the natural, manmade and hand-made, overlooked, well-made, humble, lost, and everything in between. I then start to loosely categorize. I am not strict, and I let make-believe & my memories lead the way in how I place items in a story. I am known to be fickle with some collections but not others. Do not be scared of passing on a collection you are no longer interested in, someone else will think all their Christmases (or Hanukkah for others!) have come at once.

As a stylist, casual observer, & traveler, I find my objects in many places from beaches and forests to shops, markets, dealers, auctions, sidewalks, the internet, and friends. Be prepared to be on the lookout. I like to think about things I might one day have in my possession, and more often than not they do eventually come to me.

Different things can motivate you with collecting; for me sometimes it is the space I am designing or shoot I am concepting and researching. I love history and often discover new people, ideas, movements, and tastemakers that encourage me to visit museums, historic houses, and libraries to find out more and ask questions. Once an object has more weight than a mere material possession, there is a substance & story that can be told. This gives you a home that is distinctly and beautifully yours.

ASPLENIUM BULBIFERUM

Calappa cristata, nov.

Port Jackson.

C. PHILARGIUS(L)

H. W?

How to use this book

Think of each chapter as a Cabinet of Curiosities. Although my "collections" are loosely tied and not dictated by discipline, as a museum cabinet may be, I like to consider all objects as significant and of equal importance regardless of rarity, value, or acquirement. They are based on memory, relationship, experience, the "find," the hunt, and location. How I order my collections may not make perfect sense to you, but that is the beauty & magic of being your own curator.

Some items have come through friends or family, but most of the others in this book have been acquired at no great cost, other than storage and housing, air miles, and hours of treasure hunting by me over the last twenty years of my styling career.

I want to show you how easy it is to create an emotive interior, to be surrounded by the things you love & treasure, and make any environment a reflection of you.

I encourage you to flip through these pages and enjoy the pretty pictures, use my display ideas for your own collections, be inspired to start a new collection or free-cycle one you have grown out of, start reading some good books, or use my favorite places to globetrot the world, visiting museums & shops. Enjoy!

Note: Free-cycle is to pass on pre-loved things to your friends & family, to start a new life.

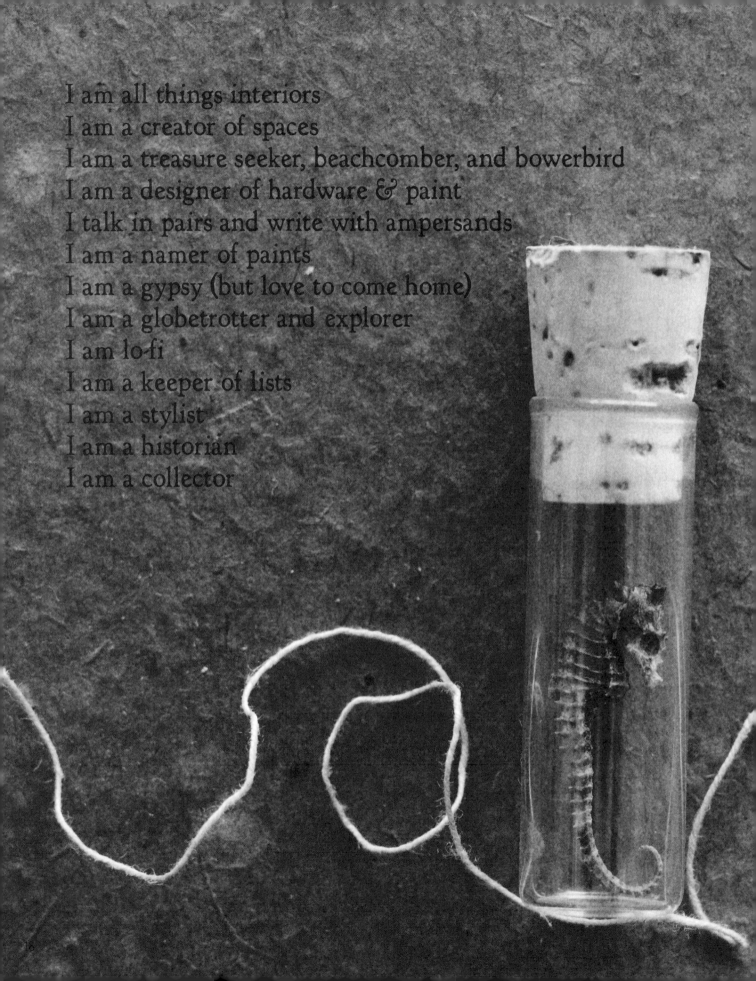

I am all things interiors
I am a creator of spaces
I am a treasure seeker, beachcomber, and bowerbird
I am a designer of hardware & paint
I talk in pairs and write with ampersands
I am a namer of paints
I am a gypsy (but love to come home)
I am a globetrotter and explorer
I am lo-fi
I am a keeper of lists
I am a stylist
I am a historian
I am a collector

Toolbag &tacklebox

These items are the basic tools & tackle you'll need to help you organize & display your collections. They are collections within themselves and, for me, contain memories & stories just like my other collections. I rely on them to create my windows at The Society inc., style a shoot, organize my things, & construct my environment. They are utilitarian, beautiful in their simplicity, and can add to your display -- and include the hand-forged exposed nail your art hangs from, vessels en masse to house your natural history finds, lead pencils sharpened with knives to write on your labels and walls, glass domes to create your mini 3D worlds, the perfect string to hold up flags, kites, lights, & anything else that needs to hang, as well as all different types & colors of tape not shy about being seen. All these supplies are an addition to your display, to be proudly revealed and not hidden away.

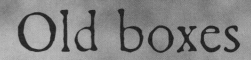

Old boxes

Old cardboard boxes hold the romance of days gone by. Not only because of the shop's stamp & labeling that might be on them but also for the box's specific shape & size, the quality & texture of the cardboard structure, the attention to the edge details, and even the hardware that holds the corner. I upcycle old boxes when they come my way to house my own collections of ribbons, bulldog clips, etc. Not only are the boxes practical but they look beautiful too.

Domes

I have an aversion to things being displayed flat on walls or shelves. Domes are a great solution – they come in lots of sizes, make it easy to change the content, and are a sculptural form in themselves.

Create small realities or dioramas with your finds that are 3D and best viewed from all angles. I like that there's a direct reference to the history of collecting in these, in that I'm using them in a very similar way to how they would have been used hundreds of years ago.

Labels

I recently bought a huge shelving system that was once part of an old Belgian hardware store. It now sits on one whole wall of my shop, The Society inc. It's the perfect shade of gray and has shelves and drawers and compartments for all the small things I hunt & gather. On some of the drawers, the old rectangular die-cut-cornered, red outlined labels still hold firm, with beautiful cursive writing, all browned & crunchy.

Many of the museums I frequent have the best old labeling and, although it is merely a form of categorizing, identifying, & organizing, I see so much beauty in a label tied to a bird skin, a simple rectangular typed & dated label on top of a corked test tube or stoppered apothecary jar. Buy old and new labels, and add your own to containers.

ROSE WATER

An excellent toilet article as an addition to face cream, lotions, etc.

THE Ideal PHARMACIES
AND 27TH AND CENTER STS
THEO. L. BAARTH, Prop.   MILWAUKEE, WIS.

Specimen

Contents-MERCHANDISE
POSTMASTER- THIS PARCEL MAY BE OPENED FOR POSTAL INSPECTION IF NECESSARY

RETURN POSTAGE GUARANTEED

−FROM−
Sibella Court
120 Walker Street
4th Floor
Chinatown 10013

To

Kramer+Kramer
Att:Sam
156 5th Ave
Suite 420
NYC 10010

SACCHARIN

A. E. PHILLIPS
PHARMACIST
SINCLAIRVILLE, NEW YORK

ence of
CONTAINS............%ALCOHOL.
E. A. PHILLIPS
PHARMACIST
SINCLAIRVILLE.   NEW YORK

FIGUES
ÉGOUTTÉES

Brut K°:
Tare   Net K°:

Pencils

I have a bundle of pencils wrapped in brown paper, all identical, a supply for a far-flung isolated place, such as the South Pole.

On one of my trips for an American magazine, I was sent to Little St Simons Island off the coast of Georgia. The story goes that, in the early 1900s, a pencil baron bought the island for the oak trees that thrived on the growing land (it's a sand-shifting island that is constantly growing). What a treat for me, for once it became apparent that the oaks were too gnarly & windswept for pencils, the island was converted into a private residence & retreat for the family.

I write my notes in pencils sharpened with knives.

Scientific paraphernalia

I have a thing for miniature things, not dollhouse things, but really small functional stuff: petri dishes, beakers, vessels, test tubes, funnels, etc.

I have bought many a vintage scientific vessel from flea markets all over the world. I use them in my own interiors both on an everyday level as well as display. They are very much a part of my own Cabinet of Curiosities as well as making an appearance in my bathroom. Old apothecary jars house decanted vitamins, glass medical jars with labels like "tongue depressors" house my cotton buds, bandages, cotton pads, & other bathroom essentials, and are a lot more sightly than the packaging of today.

Pierce[things that]

Nails, pins, tacks: hardware and stationery stores on foreign shores fascinate me and I cannot help but peruse their aisles to see what the locals are using. Hand-forged nails from Baileys, T-pins, brass dome-topped tacks, upholstery tacks both decorative & functional, dressmakers' pins, tiny bead pins, thumb tacks, etc. Each has its own personality, suitable for specific display requirements.

Tape

A tool I've used throughout my styling career and which sits just as easily at home in the third drawer. However, I have way too many varieties for one small drawer! I lean towards paper & fabric tapes in all thicknesses & colors. I'm always happy to see them sticking & securing various bits & pieces on my walls; some are even artworks on their own or a great accessory to an existing one.

Hangers
&hooks

Not just for coats & clothes, I use
coat hangers to show off everything,
including amulets, beautiful scarves,
textiles, and posters, which I hang from
a picture rail or hook or bookshelf. I
pick up old wooden & wire ones in
markets and vintage clothing stalls.
You can never have too many hooks.
Although I do have hooks on the backs
of all my doors, I use them much
more liberally, to hang sponges and
hammam towels in the bathroom, for
mirrors on the stairway. Make a feature
of them. I buy them on boards or as
singles in salvage places.

Labeled drawers

I bought my first set of labeled drawers at auction when I was in my late teens. I have always enjoyed organizing my collections in my own way, giving them all a place to live, in some state of organized chaos, and accessible when required. I keep an eye out for old shop, museum, & library furniture, including glass-fronted milliners' drawers, wooden filing cabinets, plan drawers, and pigeonholes. Many are made from oak & kauri pine, with lovely simple hardware (note: you can always change the hardware if it is not to your liking).

tins

2

Pegs

Hand-tooled, whittled, & carved, each wooden peg has its own character and function. My mother once gave me a gypsy peg: split wood with a band of thin brass at the top and tiny nails to keep the pieces together. A peg is a utilitarian object that reminds me of a time when crafts were an everyday part of life. I imagine them traveling in an old chipped enamel bowl in a colorfully painted caravan, and used to peg up many-layered skirts on a line strung between the trees by a river.

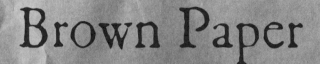

Brown Paper

You always need brown paper for something. In the shop it's a staple, and most drawers have some form of brown paper in them: envelopes of every size, letter paper, cards, rosettes, big rolls for wrapping packages, sandwich bags, tags, and postcards.

There's something endearing and comfortable about it, making you think of an old-fashioned shop where you could buy canvas buckets, yardage, chandlery, stamps, ice, and everything in between. Each purchase carefully brown paper-wrapped & tied up with string.

Fasten[tools that]

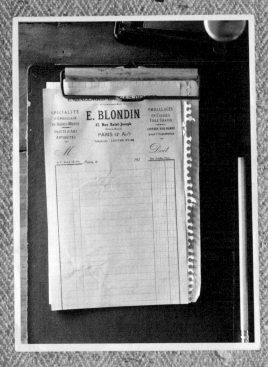

How many clips does one person need? About 5000 if you go by my books! I do not quite have that many but it may be close.

In Japan, while trawling Ito-Ya, the nine-level stationery store, I managed to come out with at least ten different styles of clips in a range of sizes from teeny weeny to huge. Irresistible. Perhaps I should have worked in a post office. Along with the clips are all the other fasteners I need, like staplers, paperclips, and clipboards.

Rope, string, & twine

I will never tire of my all-time favorite materials in the whole world. So useful, utilitarian, & natural. If I could, I would wrap the whole world in string & rope – but life might be a little too scratchy!

Regardless, balls of string, rope-wrapped furniture, string and rope to hold things up or together, let it show and let it shine (well, as much as it can).

I stayed in a yurt in an ancient fort overlooking the Aral Sea in Uzbekistan. It was made of caramel & chocolate colored felt, all held together by rope made of camel fur. It was so beautiful and romantic, and fitting for the landscape.

NATURAL FLOTSAM&JETSA

TIME IN SALTWATER, TOSSE

BEACH
COMBI

THE TIDES AND READY TO

BY THE CASUAL OBSERVER

KEEN-EYED COMBER

, WITH EVIDENCE OF ITS

ON

NG

E FOUND

R

Conchology:
the study of shells

One of my first memories is of beachcombing for shells on the wild shores of Siletto beach, on the east coast of Australia. The collection of pink kelp shells, which I gathered from huge drifts washed up on shore, sits proudly on my Cabinet of Curiosities. I have bought many fancier shells over the years and am as fascinated by the real thing as by beautiful studies, drawings, and lithographs of them, and also by things made from shells.

I am forever searching out shell museums & collections to pore over and use as inspiration for my own displays as well as to see what wonderful shapes, sizes, & colors the world's shells have to offer.

They can be divided into so many themes, studies, and families, but more often than not, I like to group them haphazardly, with no thought whatever of their scientific classification.

An overscaled shell chandelier invites you to stop and sit down. It adds a 3D element to an otherwise blank wall.

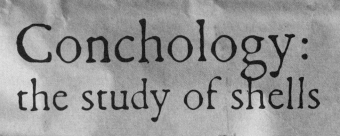

⫸⟶

Shells & seaforms are found in many shapes & sizes: some collected
singularly on an island beach, many collected all at once after a storm, an
arrangement picked up for a few dollars at a flea market, or dug out from
the sands of Tulum in Mexico. Arrange them together, on a shelf, or
mantel. Bring in different vessels, domes, & bottles to house your finds.
Add elements like books or leftover cardboard packaging to introduce
height & color.

Driftwood

I saw a lookout, which I expect belonged to a builder /
surfer, on the coast of Washington State, just south of
the giant redwood forests. I would rather refer to it as a
pirate ship: with its ladders, platforms, and flagpole made
out of huge driftwood logs and all the way down to the
smaller easier-to-pick-up kind. The perfect sea-starched
& bleached grays, lightwood feel, soft & smooth edges
of driftwood have inspired many a craft project as
well as provided a well-deserved oceanside sit down or
wave lookout.

A simple solution for what to do with that driftwood you
picked up. Use as a table runner for harvest decoration
and then as a trivet for when the roast chicken &
vegetables arrive – yum!

Loofahs,sponges,&pumice

I can't resist the different shapes & textures of natural sponges, hand-knitted loofahs, and pumice: tear-shaped, jet black, or the common gray, imperfectly round but manmade in shape. I have come across so many on seaside vacations, and in places where hammams & bathhouses are part of the weekly ritual. Mostly found in markets, I picked up my most recent favorite loofahs in Aleppo, Syria, around the corner from the ancient olive oil soap factory. All round and coarse, a stack of them was a must (one was just not enough). On a trip to Greece I found several large white pumice pieces, rounded edges and one painted side, floating in the waters off Santorini. Being a super sleuth, I figure these must have been part of a wall (hence the paint on one side) washed away by the sea. Make your selection of pumice, both decorative and useful. Let your family and guests scrub away life's wear & tear, and display the different colors and origins of stacked pumice on a handy bathroom shelf or in vessels of different shapes & sizes.

Oysters

Bell'occhio, a favorite shop in San Francisco, sells, among other things, handcrafted French papier-mâché boxes of fruits, nuts, shells, and the like. I have one in the shape of an oyster. I love the romance of oysters, and have been known to ask the very obliging waitstaff at Balthazar to wash my dozen mini Kumamoto shells after a particularly pleasant lunch as a memento. The shape for me is iconic, irregular, and one of nature's naturally crafted vessels. The color varies so much from shore to shore, and inspired, both in color & patina, one of my paints, aptly named "Oyster Grey."

Use your seashore finds (or restaurant mementoes) for salt and pepper, adding a textural and story element to the table. You can use them to dictate a color palette of soft pewters, sun-bleached whites, & inky grays (or not).

Pebbles&sea-tossed stones

I collect these on my globetrotting and
beachcombing adventures, and am very
particular about shape, feel, & color.
Smooth, gray, and egg-shaped are my
favorite; add a white line and I'm over
the moon. It's rare for me not to have
a stone handy as a paperweight, trivet,
doorstop, or a styling tool. They line
my stairs and my bathtub and sink, and
hold memories of vacations, people, and
watery endeavors.

Seahorses &other watery creatures

My brother Chris photographed a man who builds ships in bottles on particularly stormy days when fishing is a no-go. Other than solving the mystery of these bottled gems, Chris was given a gift of a seahorse. It's in its dried form, but has the elements of illustration, smooth and rigid at the same time.

My own collection includes one that is so small (about half an inch long) it had its own corked bottle. Others I rescued from Chinese medicine shops while I was living in NYC's Chinatown.

Recently, a woman came into my store and told me that they were a fertility symbol, with a very high success rate among her friends & family.

I now stock porcelain ones in my shop – in case you are in need of some help!

Deep-sea magic in a jar. Place it on the windowsill to make it all the more beautiful as the sun shines through this fabric interpretation of a jellyfish.

[NEXT PAGE]
Lay out your finds on an open handmade book, add some labels with origin, date, etc. of your find, pin if desired.

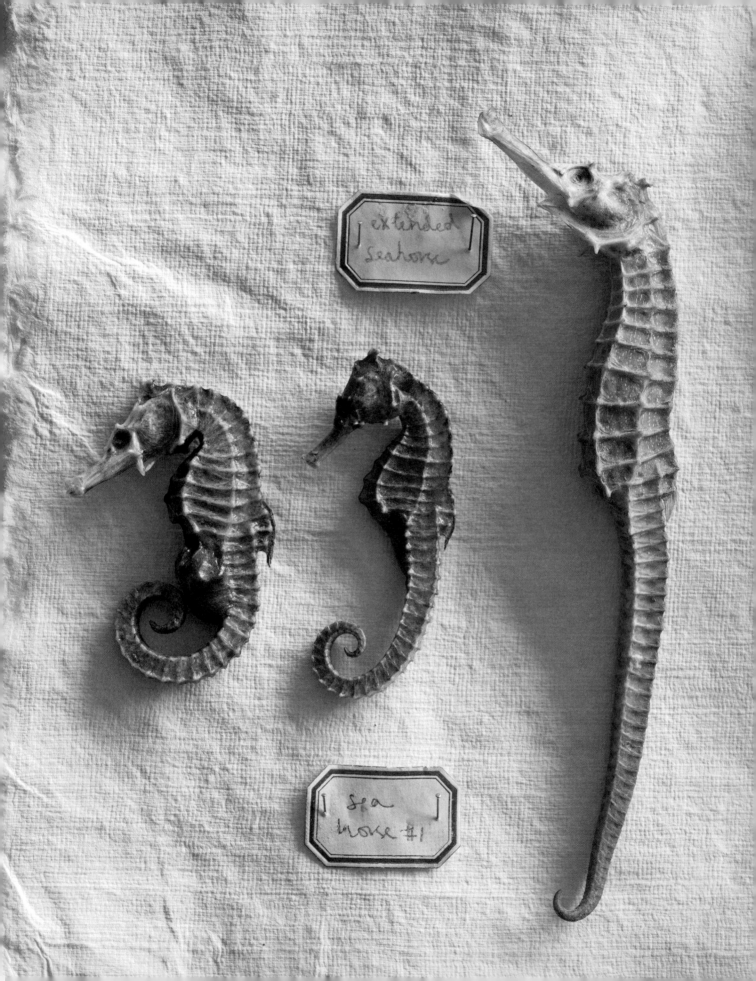

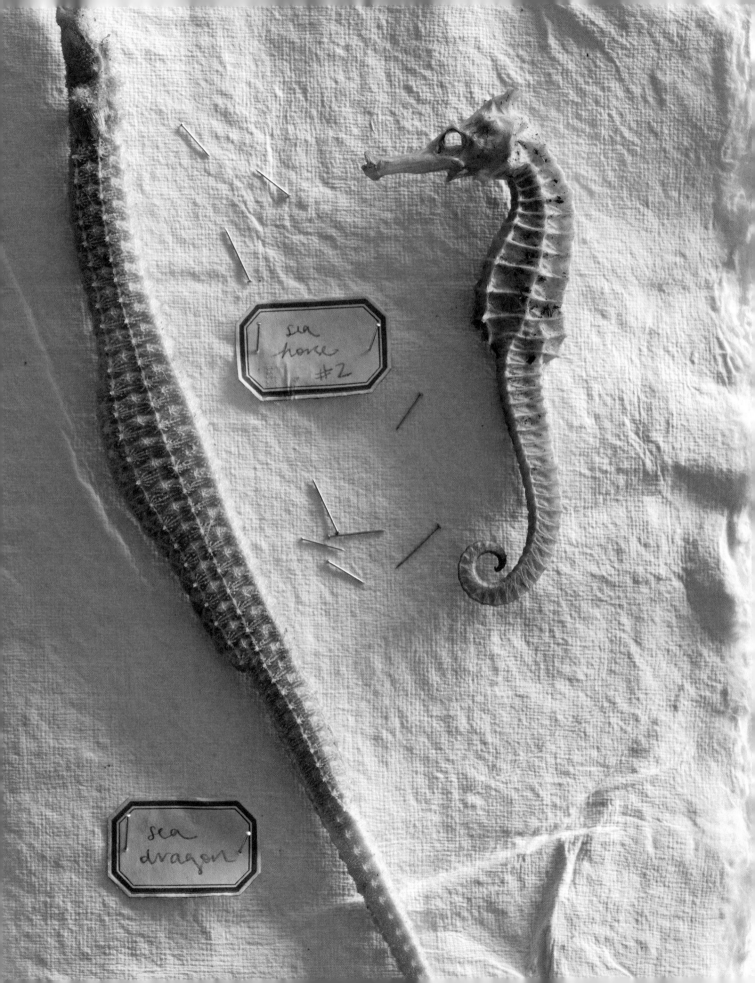

AN ORDINARY OBJECT, FOU
A STRAND OF SEQUINS, A
THREADS,&BUTTONS. THI

OBJET T

WITH PLEASURE, IN A LON
OR AT THE BOTTOM OF A
FADED&FRAYED, PRE-LOVE
ORIGIN: FRANCE, FOUND O

D.

AND-STITCHED FLOWER,

S DISCOVERED,

ROUVÉ

ABANDONED ATTIC

ADED OPERA PURSE;

& GLORIOUS.

ECT

2

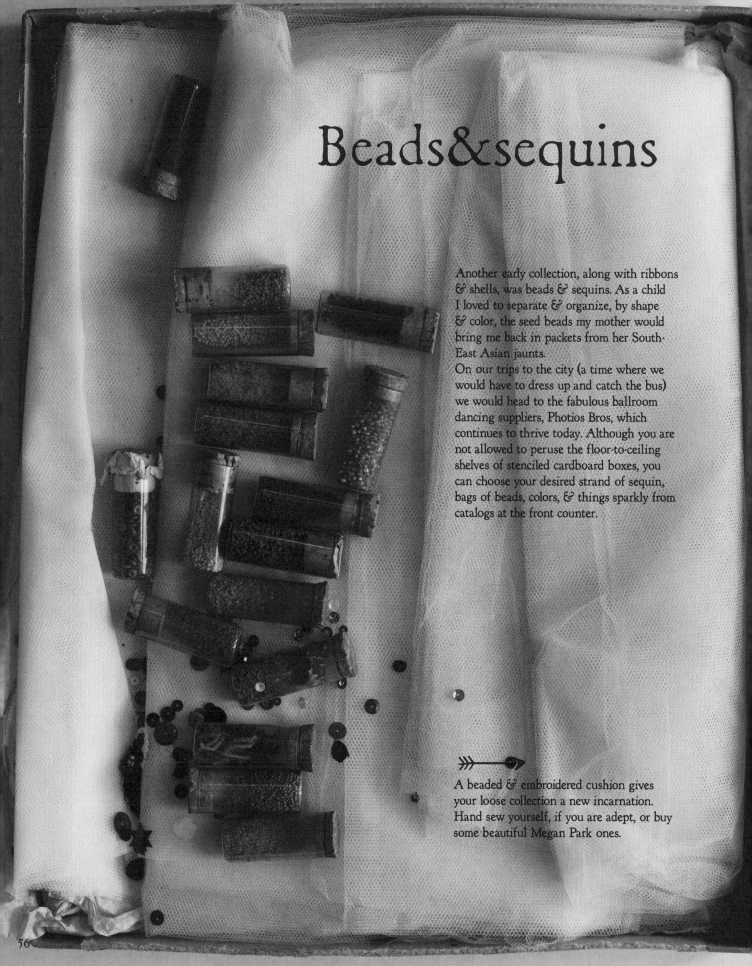

Beads&sequins

Another early collection, along with ribbons & shells, was beads & sequins. As a child I loved to separate & organize, by shape & color, the seed beads my mother would bring me back in packets from her South-East Asian jaunts.

On our trips to the city (a time where we would have to dress up and catch the bus) we would head to the fabulous ballroom dancing suppliers, Photios Bros, which continues to thrive today. Although you are not allowed to peruse the floor-to-ceiling shelves of stenciled cardboard boxes, you can choose your desired strand of sequin, bags of beads, colors, & things sparkly from catalogs at the front counter.

A beaded & embroidered cushion gives your loose collection a new incarnation. Hand sew yourself, if you are adept, or buy some beautiful Megan Park ones.

Buttons

I have a wooden box with compartments for my own buttons, sorted into colors, and easy to find when one has popped off my shirt or coat and is nowhere to be found. Although there are some very serious collections of buttons out there, mine is not one of them. It's a hodgepodge of my own, my mother's, her mother's and her mother's. A little timeline of history in itself in ways of fashion, new technologies, and availability of materials. Of course today I like the leather buttons that look like knots, tiny irregular mother of pearl ones, very plain calico-covered ones, and the like.

[NEXT PAGE]
Spell out your desired message, attach to walls or floors. You could use pins or nails, glue or double-stick tape to attach, depending on traffic areas and surface.

Haberdashery

I opened a store so I could sell old haberdashery things (and other globetrotting finds & treasures). I have many a fond memory of haberdashery visits while growing up. My mother was great at sewing, so we would often be matching thread to fabric and buying a quarter yard of material (she made beautiful quilts), plus ribbons for my pigtails.

My version of a haberdasher's store is more nineteenth century than 1970s: all things attached to paper; sets of ten mother of pearl buttons; glass-topped dressmakers' pins; thread on wooden spools with typography paper ends; fabric tape measures and other needs; needles in tin casing; tailor's chalk.

All these things make up my sewing kit, and give me great pleasure whenever I need to mend or make something.

My threads often look like a tangled mess; put them in a loop on wire or string in colorways for ease & organization. They look so pretty; keep them out as decoration.

Hands

A boyfriend and I had a secret language. When we needed to tell each other "I love you," we would press our palms together. We thought of getting smaller versions (of the outline of each other's hands) on our shoulders so when we were sleeping at night, side by side, our palms would be pressed together.

I no longer have that boyfriend but am left with a fascination for hands. The protective hand of Fatima, a French door knock of a hand clasping a ball, illustrations of sign language and shadow puppets, hands cast in metal and carved out of graphite to write with, wooden artists' hands, the outline of a loved one's hand on the wall in pencil, the wire outlines you push into gloves to maintain their shape, and even the simple saying of "fingers crossed."

Old-fashioned souvenirs

I think the word "souvenir" gets a really bad rap. I want to conjure up all the romance of travel and the idea of coming into the port of a place that was so foreign, the desire to take a piece as a memento was too strong to deny. Souvenirs were often made by local artisans for visiting tourists (also a word that gets a hard time).

Things like shell cameos from the Amalfi Coast, Native American beaded purses from Niagara Falls, pincushions out of conch shells from the Bahamas. A little kitsch, maybe, but the set of bamboo-handled knives & forks with "Surfers Paradise" hand-painted on each handle that my great friends Donna & Will gave me many years ago have long been treasured and many times used.

I love a mad mantel. Play with scale, color palette, texture, & materials. If anything, make people smile. Here souvenirs are the theme: temple sticks from Laos, a paper grass parrot by Anna-Wili and a geranium (one of my favorite old-fashioned flowers) sitting on cardboard discs, scraps from my shop, green pom-poms, and some sea-tossed pebbles from a faraway shore. A 3D reflection of my travels & me!

Wherever I travel, I buy a
version of a panama hat. It
is part of my outfit and now
I have many. On my most
recent trip, I visited Ecuador,
the home of the panama hat.

Shaving mirrors

These look great alone or en masse. I pick them up all over the world. They fold flat, come on a stand, and are mostly round, oval, or shield shaped. The original idea was as a traveling mirror to hang or stand alone on a dresser or convenient surface, such as a sand dune, side of a mountain, campaign table, train bunker, back of the door, or tree branch, depending on your destination.

The other option is the freestanding kind, with an adjustable angle. Not as practical for adventures but they look great standing against your existing mirror or in a dressing room, by a bed, a specially made shelf, or the like.

I most recently found a round one about ten inches in diameter with a wonky wire stand, in a dusty antique shop in Ho Chi Minh City, slightly neglected, but lovely in all its tattered-ness.

ANIMALS
WITH
QUILLS

SEA
URCHINS
BIRDS
PORCUPINES
ECHIDNAS
ANTEATERS
HEDGEHOGS

CREATURES THAT WALK & F

AND THEIR VARIOUS BODY

ZOOLO
ENTOM

THE REINTERPRETATION O

HOUSES THEY MAKE; THE F

THEY LEAVE BEHIND FOR U

Antlers&trophies

Although I am very anti-hunting and concerned
about extinction, I continue to have a somewhat
romantic view of colonialism and hunting safaris.
The idea of the hunting lodge with cavernous
rooms, either in the east of India or the cold craggy
mountains of Scotland, walls crammed with trophy
heads, jostling for pride of place.
There's nothing like the find of a shed antler while
traversing the countryside. It feels such a score to
cart home. I would love to be in the country of
roaming elk, and to one day stumble upon an elk's
antler, or even a pair!

←———⧸⧸⧸

A papier-mâché menagerie makes a transitional room
a little fun. Attach them low & high so each has
room for its own personality.

Vintage hunting photos found in
India hang together, reminiscent of a
lodge. Add a surprise element to stop
it taking itself too seriously.

HOME GUARDS, AHMEDABAD.
JAMALPUR WARD.
29TH. NOVEMBER 1948.

Bird's nests, eggs, & skulls

I have always loved exploring in nature, and picking up treasures as I ramble. It's a rare day to find unusual eggs and skulls but, after strong winds, an eagle eye can find a grounded nest. I often have nests perched on top of cupboards, on my mantel, or just sitting on a block of wood somewhere. If your searching hours are limited, you can visit your local natural history museum for inspiration and make your own nest with twigs & sticks.

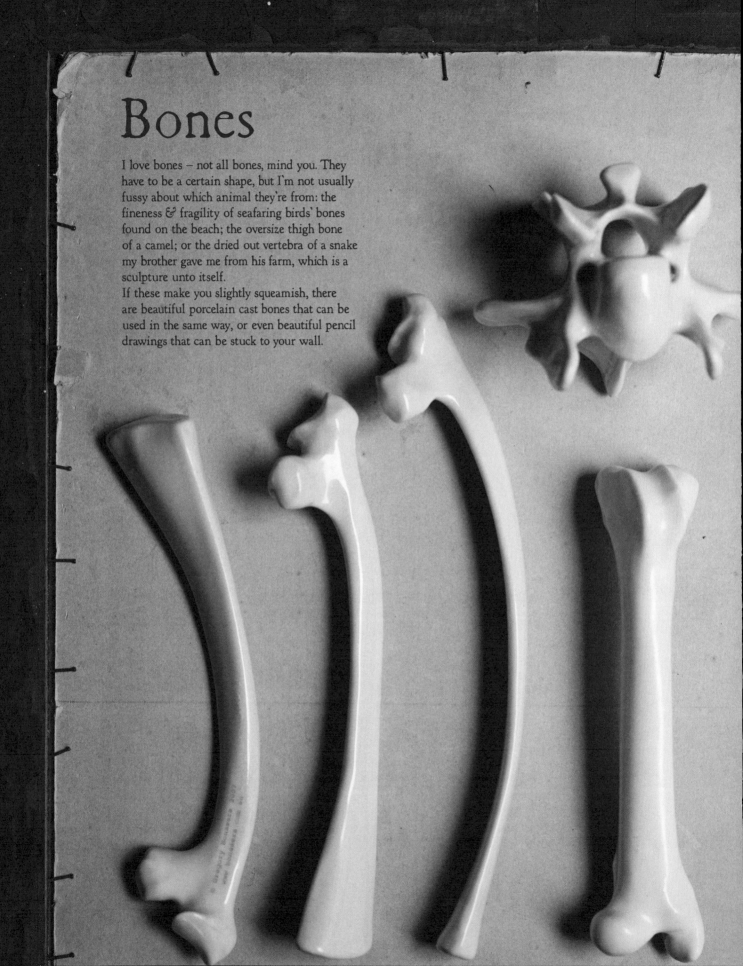

Bones

I love bones – not all bones, mind you. They
have to be a certain shape, but I'm not usually
fussy about which animal they're from: the
fineness & fragility of seafaring birds' bones
found on the beach; the oversize thigh bone
of a camel; or the dried out vertebra of a snake
my brother gave me from his farm, which is a
sculpture unto itself.

If these make you slightly squeamish, there
are beautiful porcelain cast bones that can be
used in the same way, or even beautiful pencil
drawings that can be stuck to your wall.

Feathers

I have never lost the thrill of the discovery of a fallen feather. Lorikeet, kookaburra, seafaring birds, blue jay – though I'm yet to find a red cardinal. I look for stripes, colors, neutrals, big & small, dotted, white, and jet inky black.

My mother told me many times that I was an angel with dreadlocks & mottled wings! I find a lot of feathers and am also given many by friends. I am sure this is so I can replace the fallen ones and still be able to fly. As well as single bird feathers, I have many things made out of feathers – arrows, darts, paintbrushes, fans, hair ornaments, and headdresses.

Winged: dragonflies, butterflies, and cicadas

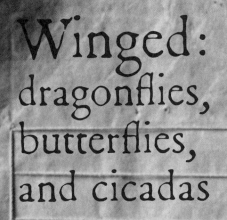

I can't remember when my fascination with things that fly began, but perhaps it was when my dad introduced my brothers & me to all the summer cicadas, and the different noises they make. We would wait for the season to start and the cicadas to emerge from the ground.

At some point my dad also had a stint at catching & pinning butterflies – I loved his boxed collection. One of my top five list of things to see is the migration of the Monarch butterflies when they amass on the Californian coast in Big Sur on their way south.

I remember the first time I visited Deyrolle in Paris on rue du Bac, a most wonderful shop that is truly a Cabinet of Curiosities. The smell, the greeting at the top of the stairs by a polar bear – or was it a grizzly bear, or lion?

I bought a beautiful collection of butterflies and a rhino bug at the NYC Pier Antiques Show. Years later, when I was getting them restored by my now good friend, Jessica Grindstaff at Evolution's entomological department, I found out that they were original Deyrolle pieces, much to my delight.

Nothing is more magical than the American Museum of Natural History butterfly conservatory, a stroll of fancy through a room of live, beautifully colored butterflies. One year I had just finished a Jo Malone shoot and was covered in one of her moisturizers.

As I wandered through the live exhibit, Paper Kites, attracted to the scents, landed on my shoulders and stayed the duration of my visit. Now, that's magic.

If you can't get your hands on the real thing, buy wrapping paper and carefully cut out butterflies, pin to a board with entomological pins, label as desired.

Quills
&sea urchins

Depending on the animal they derive from, quills come in such dramatically different shapes. (There are six, see my list.)

At my shop, The Society inc., I have glass apothecary jars full of sea urchin quills in shades of purple, dusky pink, and deep eggplant, often with white-ringed tips. They feel and look like unglazed porcelain, and when knocked together, make a beautiful musical chime-y sound.

I admire the stripey and color (and sharp protective) elements of quills, both from urchins & the porcupine families. I have loose bundles & jars of them in many shapes & sizes, as my fascination doesn't seem to wane.

>>>———>

A lampshade made from quills becomes part of a picture; a frame simply leaning against the wall with a selection of objects to give it some friends. Perfect for the top of a chest or in a corner as a little beacon of welcome.

[NEXT PAGE]
An array of scientific vessels house various quills, easily accessed to be handled and admired.

TINCT
APOTH
&ALCH

THE TOOLS USED TO MIX&
WEIGH&MEASURE; MIXTUR
AND THE VESSELS THAT H

Atelier

Pastels, paints, inks, and dyes: the joy of finding an old artists' set of partly used colors. I love what the palette suggests of its previous owner; often the box or housing alone is enough to entice. I based my color palette of red & orange tones, aptly named "Atelier," on late nineteenth century Paris, where a shop on rue de Seine in St Germain used to sell artists' supplies. Known affectionately as Père Tanguy, the owner supplied the likes of Cézanne, Gauguin, Seurat, and van Gogh (who painted his portrait at least three times). I can just see his shop filled with apothecary jars full of ochers, aquamarine, pomegranate rinds, crushed up shells, cochineal, matta, indigo, snail ink, gold leaf, shellac, brushes, gesso, plinths, stools that twist, and bottles of linseed oil. I have since been obsessed with all the unusual and necessary things you find in an artist's studio.
Père Tanguy ran a small gallery on the side and often traded paintings for pigments, which jam-packed his walls alongside his collection of ukiyo-e Japanese prints. It was a salon of its day – a place of conversation and ideas over a couple of glasses of absinthe.

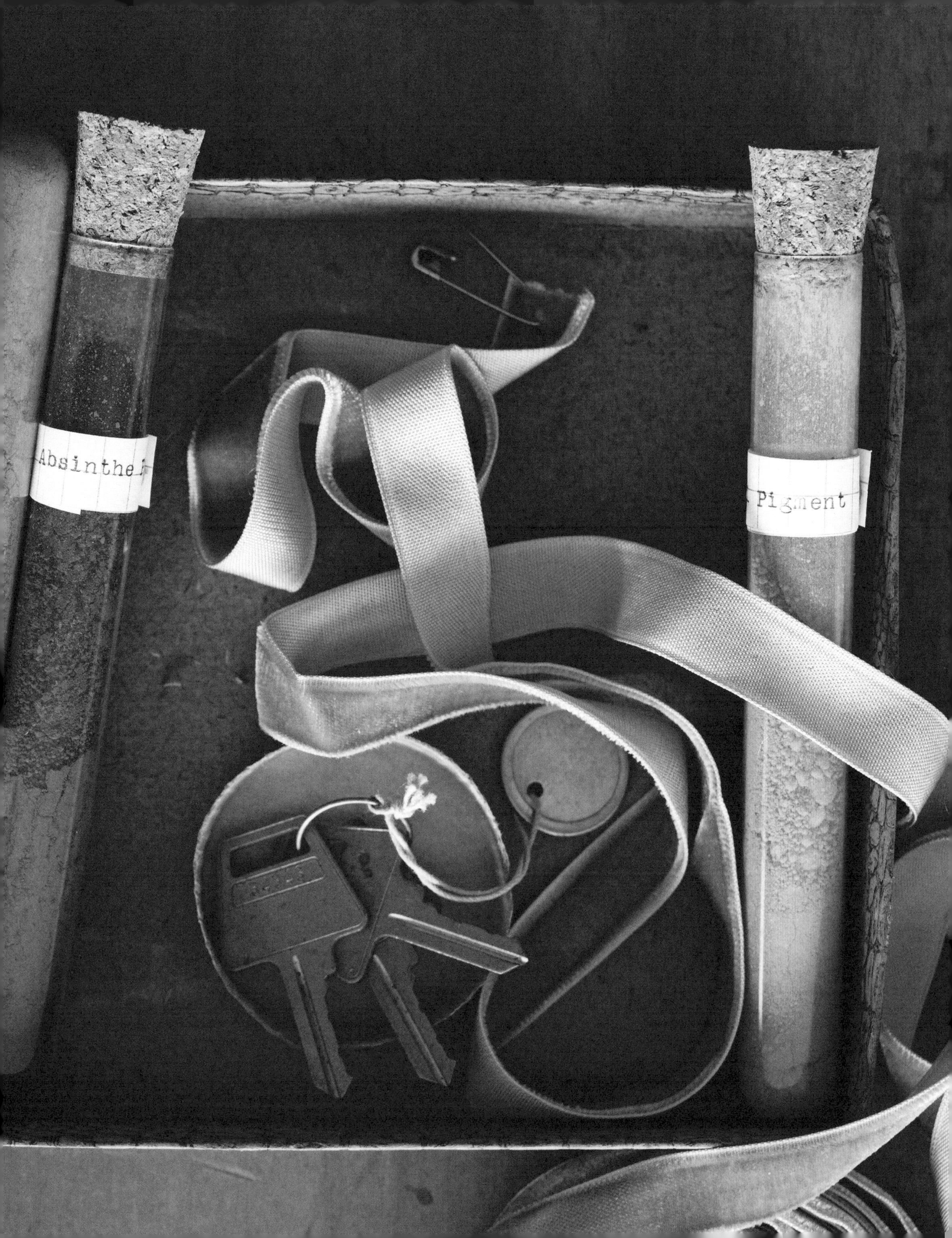
Absinthe
Pigment

Brushes

Even before I had
a paint range, I had a
rather large collection
of brushes that my
antique dealer friend
Alan sourced for me.
I think about the
care that painters,
signwriters, and barbers
take of their real bristle
brushes, treating them
with respect so they last
a lifetime.

[NEXT PAGE]
My collection hangs on the
underside of the shelf above
a doorway, creating a lovely
threshold. The brushes are
attached with small brass cup
& eye hooks, easy to take down
for closer examination & use.
A couple of stores (New York
Central Art Supply and Sam
Flax) have brushes I can't resist
– specialized and handmade
ones made from animal fur,
feathers, bamboo, wood, and
other lovely materials.

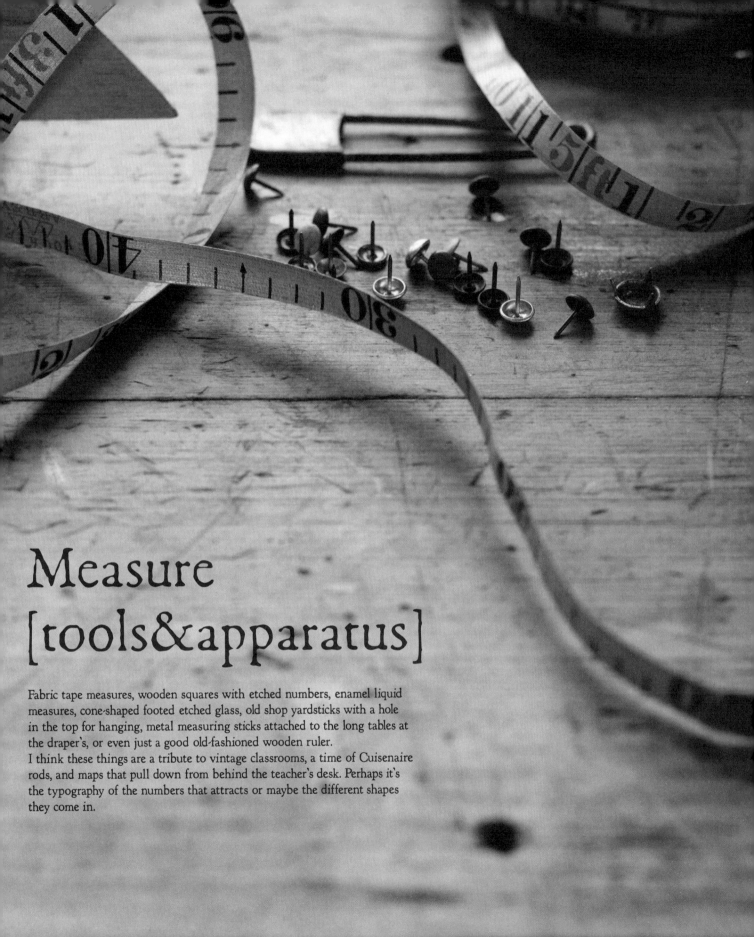

Measure
[tools&apparatus]

Fabric tape measures, wooden squares with etched numbers, enamel liquid measures, cone-shaped footed etched glass, old shop yardsticks with a hole in the top for hanging, metal measuring sticks attached to the long tables at the draper's, or even just a good old-fashioned wooden ruler.

I think these things are a tribute to vintage classrooms, a time of Cuisenaire rods, and maps that pull down from behind the teacher's desk. Perhaps it's the typography of the numbers that attracts or maybe the different shapes they come in.

A simple set of shapes for drawing & measuring, now obsolete but the combination is just right, with the soft of the fabric surveyors' tape, the hard of the wooden rulers, and the round & right angles of the various tools.

3.

Bottles[mini]

One day (hopefully soon) I am going to have my own perfume and home fragrance range. When this happens, I have all I need on hand for inspiration. I have a vision that my perfect scent (possibly rose-based) will hang on a beautiful chain lanyard or leather tie around the neck in a miniature corked bottle, on the ready for when you need some freshening up. In the meantime I have many small bottles that I adore for their sheer tininess and their past lives: some held perfume samples, some Chinese medicine, and others perhaps dosages of poison.

The amber shielded bottles hold an air of mystery, and a hint of the exotic. Although they appear medicinal, give them a new life and use them to house your things: rings, cotton buds, coins, or even paperclips.

ACETATE
CANTHARIDE

POISON

Aconitin.

اكونيتين

ANTIPYRINE

WAYS OF ACQUIRING & EXPANDING A COLLECTION

EXCHANGE WITH FELLOW COLLECTORS, MONGERS, & LOCAL FISHERMEN, DEALERS ABROAD, MAIL ORDER FROM NATURAL HISTORY SPECIALISTS, PERSONAL EXPEDITIONS, EXPLORING, HIRED COLLECTORS WHO WORK REMOTE PARTS OF THE WORLD, DONATIONS, PURCHASES FROM SETTLERS, BUCCANEERS, & MISSIONARIES

FROM WARD'S NATURAL HISTORY ESTABLISHMENT OF NEW YORK, MR G. RICE'S CURIOSITIES ON GEORGE ST, MRS J.S. PALMER & SON, FURRIER & TAXIDERMISTS ON HUNTER ST

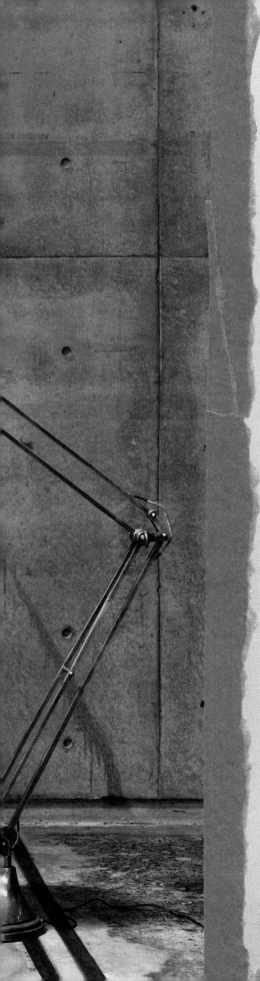

Samples &swatches

I opened a box at my storage space recently and found my samples of fake grass and fake snow. It reminded me of my years in New York City building sets. Then I put it back on the shelf, to look forward to the next time I open it. I have lots of samples. I blame it on my job but I do love to see the color or texture variations of the same thing in a small size.

Since the days of traveling salesmen, we have had samples & swatch boards. It's always lovely to come upon an old bead, ribbon, or lace board. At the indigo dyer's house in Kyoto, he let me pore over his great-grandfather's indigo kimono sample books: mulberry paper, thick with fabric squares, and hand-bound. This was extra special.

My paint palettes are swatched out on long drops of brown paper. Here "Tradewinds" becomes part of the installation and more art than example.

[NEXT PAGE]
I picked up this nail sample board from Kiosk. I like that it is not flat, does not need to be framed (as I like to take out the nails), and sits happily with a grouping of frames & ephemera.

EL YELLOW   WINE   SKY BLUE   BOTTLE

LD GOLD   MAROON   SAXE BLUE   CREA

ORANGE   LAVENDER   ROYAL BLUE   SUNT

SALMON   HELIOTROPE   NAVY BLUE   LIGHT

PINK   VIOLET   LIGHT GREEN   PRINCES

ROSE   DUSKY   PEACOCK GREEN   DARK

RED   MASTIC   MID GREEN   BLA

THE TRADITIONAL TRADE

BLACKSMITHS, & SILVERSMIT

SMITH
& TINK

FUNCTIONAL PIECES FROM

AND MERCHANTS WHO SC

FROM TOWN TO VILLAGE T

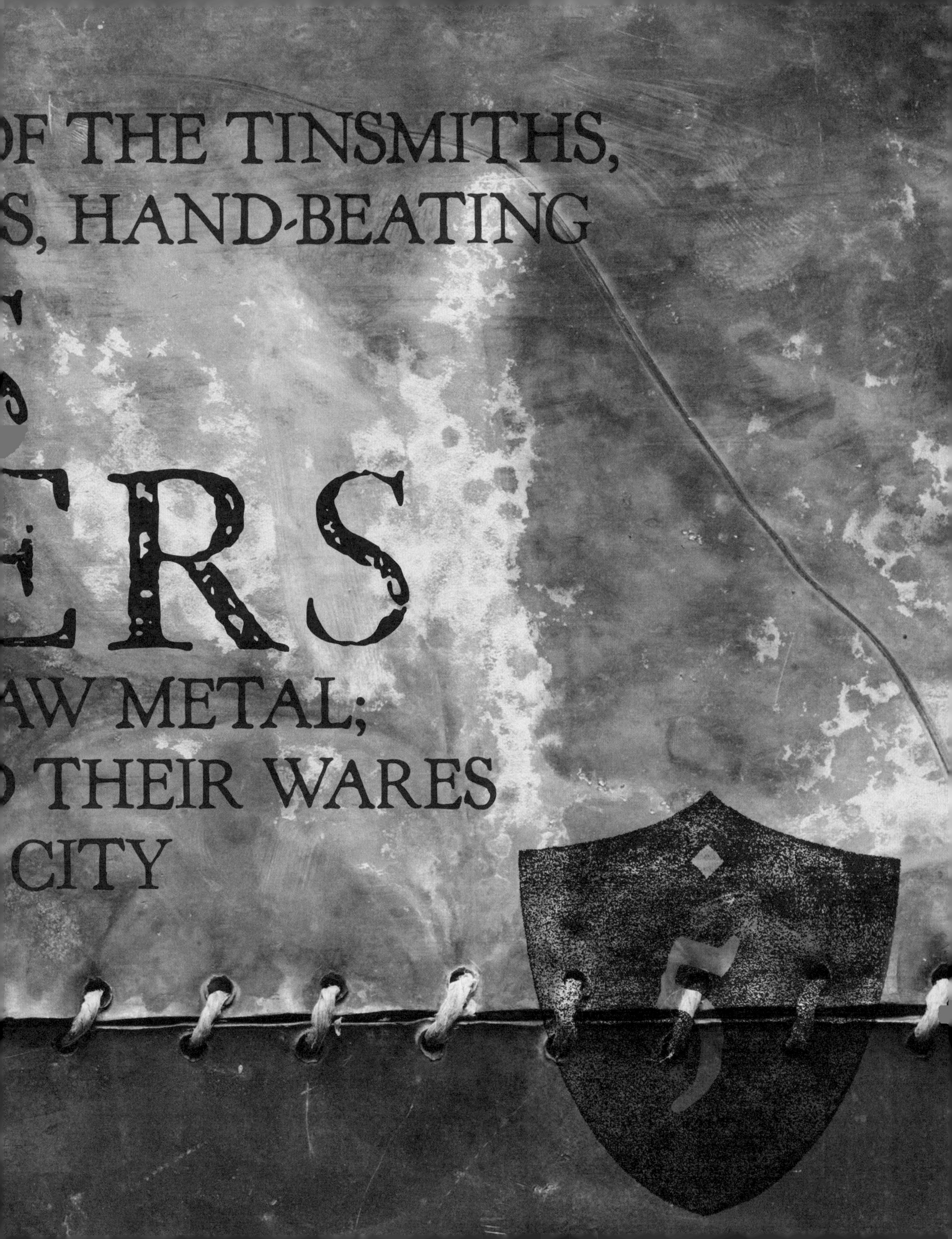

OF THE TINSMITHS,
S, HAND-BEATING

RS

AW METAL;
D THEIR WARES
CITY

Lights that hang&clip

NAMES
CICADAS

DOUBLE
DRUMMER
TOM THUMB
GREEN GROCER
YELLOW MONDAY
BLACK PRINCE
CHERRY NOSE
FLOURY BAKER

I'm going to say that this came about because of my total dislike for downlights. I do not like to be in a spotlight, blinded by misdirected lighting. Everyone looks fabulous in soft ambient lighting, so why not make a prettier & happier world? I have picked up old & new lights the world over and love the immediacy of clipping them onto a shelf or chair, or hanging where I want them to hang. Note: Don't be deterred by different voltages, make friends with an electrician who can MacGyver them to suit your country code.

⫸⟶

Wire up your found shades with extra-long cords so that you can move with ease to any setting you create.

Stamped&official

A girlfriend of mine once asked where I hide all my ugly stuff. I believe that nothing has to be ugly. Rather than grab the first thing I see, I'll keep an eye out for something old, well-made, and considered in its design and material. This applies to hole punches, receipt pins, string holders, tape dispensers, and the like. While looking for them, I keep coming across rubber stamps (although not always made of rubber). The irregularity appeals to me and they have become a staple at The Society inc. We do get some made, always the ones you use the inkpad with. In Hanoi I watched a man carve my name & address out of wood in English, backwards, circular and about an inch high for each letter. He presented me with the most beautiful wooden business stamp plus bright red ink & pad. I was very happy — it felt like an incredibly special gift.

EMPIRE TYPEWRITER SUPPLIES
PTY. LTD.
188-194 GEORGE STREET, SYDNEY
PHONE: BW 2375 (5 Lines)

RAYMAC CO. PTY. LTD.

270 ELIZABETH ST.

SYDNEY .

Not only are you recycling & saving some room in landfill, but you are bringing back the past with well-made, well-designed machinery that continues to be relevant & functional in our digital age. These are lovely to look at, and feel nostalgic to touch: a time of pencil skirts & hairpins.

Sibella Court

THE SOCIETY INC

18 Stewart Stre

PADDINGTON NS

POST
AUS

Stencils

I squirrel these out from country antique stores, flea markets, hardware and stationery stores. Many are old handmade metal ones, some are single letters & numbers, others the names or initials from working farms or a crude form of labeling or maker's mark. An old-fashioned way of branding your logo. I find I use these in my own commercial designs as well as around my house and shop.

To me they have dual functionality. Firstly, they can be a display piece in themselves, hung on the wall with small nails you can see (try to use hand-forged ones), either as a collection or on their own as a piece of art.

Secondly, they can be used for what they were created for. With either a spray paint or a stipple brush, you can transform a simple piece of burlap by stenciling on an ampersand then stitching into a square. I have zhuzhed many a chair by stenciling a number or word onto it.

Create a console with a stenciled box – all it takes are some old stencils, spray paint, and an afternoon to spare. This one is turned on its side to reveal its fab stenciled base.

I stenciled this old canvas bag to keep my pegs in. Hang it on your line ready for use.

[NEXT PAGE]
Lay your stencils out flat on a table as a surface. Don't be timid, put your vase or other objects right on top of them.

EQUIPMENT YOU MAY NEED FOR A FIELD TRIP & DISPLAY

FLOWER PRESSES &
HERBARIA
SPECIMEN JARS
RAIN BOOTS (OR A
SENSIBLE SHOE)
CLEAR BAGS WITH
SECURE TOPS
TEST TUBES WITH
CORK TOPS
PETRI DISHES
SKETCHBOOK &
PENCIL
ARTISTS' ROLL
SHEARS & SCISSORS OR
A KNIFE THAT FOLDS
BELT WITH POCKETS
OR CARGO PANTS
BUTTERFLY NET
ALARM CLOCK (FOR
EARLY MORNING
FORAGING)
STICKY TAPE (A
COLLECTION IN
ITSELF)
BOXES WITH CLEAR
TOPS
LABELS & TAGS
PITH HELMET
ENTOMOLOGICAL PINS
ARSENIC
CAMERA
VASCULUM
SMALL TROWEL
MAGNIFYING GLASS
PAPER TAPE
ALBUM

Scissors

Scissors from Vietnam, my great-grandmother's pinking shears, tiny, tiny cord-covered Japanese ones, Chinese kitchen scissors —you name them, I seem to have acquired them. The other day I bought three pairs of wallpaper scissors with long blades that remind me of the legs of a wetlands wading bird. Some of mine come in boxes and others are wrapped in paper so as not to pierce you after purchase, but all of them remind me of a place, a trade, a specialized task that always has to do with working with your hands and focusing on what you are working on: cutting a pattern, cooking (I cut my herbs with scissors, call me lazy if you wish), measuring off a yard, wallpapering, etc.

There is no reason why utilitarian tools should not be beautiful; these are for use and display.

[NEXT PAGE]
Lay scissors out for display and, when necessary, easy reach for the task at hand (perhaps out of reach of small children!).

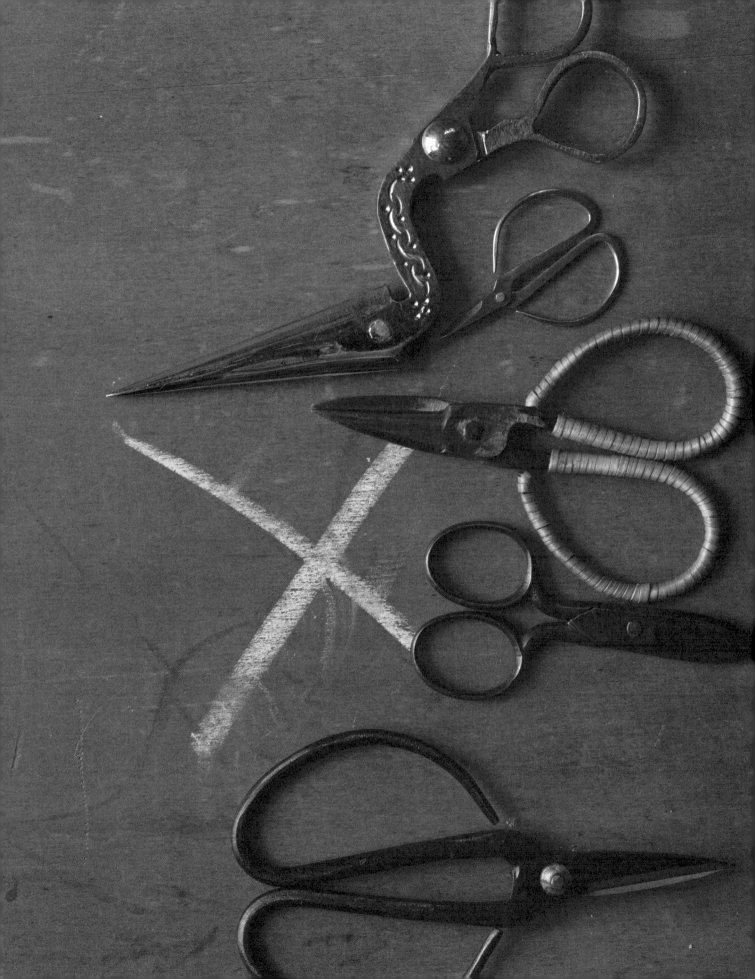

Utensils

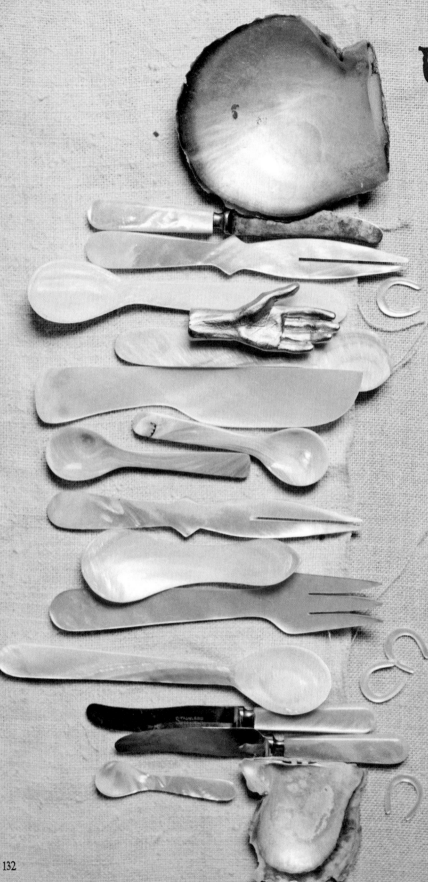

I am one of those people who has everything you could possibly need in a kitchen, but buy only what is aesthetically pleasing. I like to display my array on hanging racks – so it's a wooden handle over a plastic one for me.

You can gauge my trips by the variety and material of hand-carved spoons I have: made from wood, shell, mother of pearl, snails, bamboo, and horn from various ports around the world.

Many of my early memories are of cooking with my mother, sifting flour, beating eggs, all the simple chores of youth. The hand utensils she had now hang, full of childhood memories, on my utensil rack, for all to see: whisks, wooden spoons, flour sifts, cake testers, mushroom brushes, wire cooling racks, and colanders.

⟫⟫⟫⟶

Some old spoon molds made from plastic are simply taped up on the wall. The ugly side of a refrigerator is covered in brown paper both as disguise and a useful place for a to-do list.

buy Smeg black matt fridge
200
50
chris —
chips, chicken burger
& coke
+ 45
+ 115
belle —
salad
protein shake
V. B.

Vintage hardware

I've had the pleasure of going through the floors of foundry & decorative hardware P.E. Guerin est. 1857: drawers spilling with molds, casts, one-offs, discontinued drawer pulls, and faucets. Many people would not take a second look at forgotten or superseded hardware, but for me it holds as much wonder as a treasure chest. I have used inspiration from my own collection of aging wood and tarnished metal to create my functional hardware range. The expertise of old tradesmen – forgers and tinkers and smiths – has been lost as handmade became machine-made and mass-produced. I want to bring back the time when the pieces you bought felt as if someone had whittled them or sharpened them to imperfection with their own hands. The goods they made were so lovely – hardware that should be displayed, not hidden. If you can't afford to renovate, or don't want to, these most simple of things will transform a space.

FABRIC BY THE YARD ON L
ROLLED OUT, MEASURED, A

DRAPE
&MILLS

TAILORS' SCISSORS; THE W
TEXTILES&CLOTH; THE LO
THAT AWAITED THEIR DEI
FRENCH SILKS, VELVETS, G
ALL THINGS MILLINERY

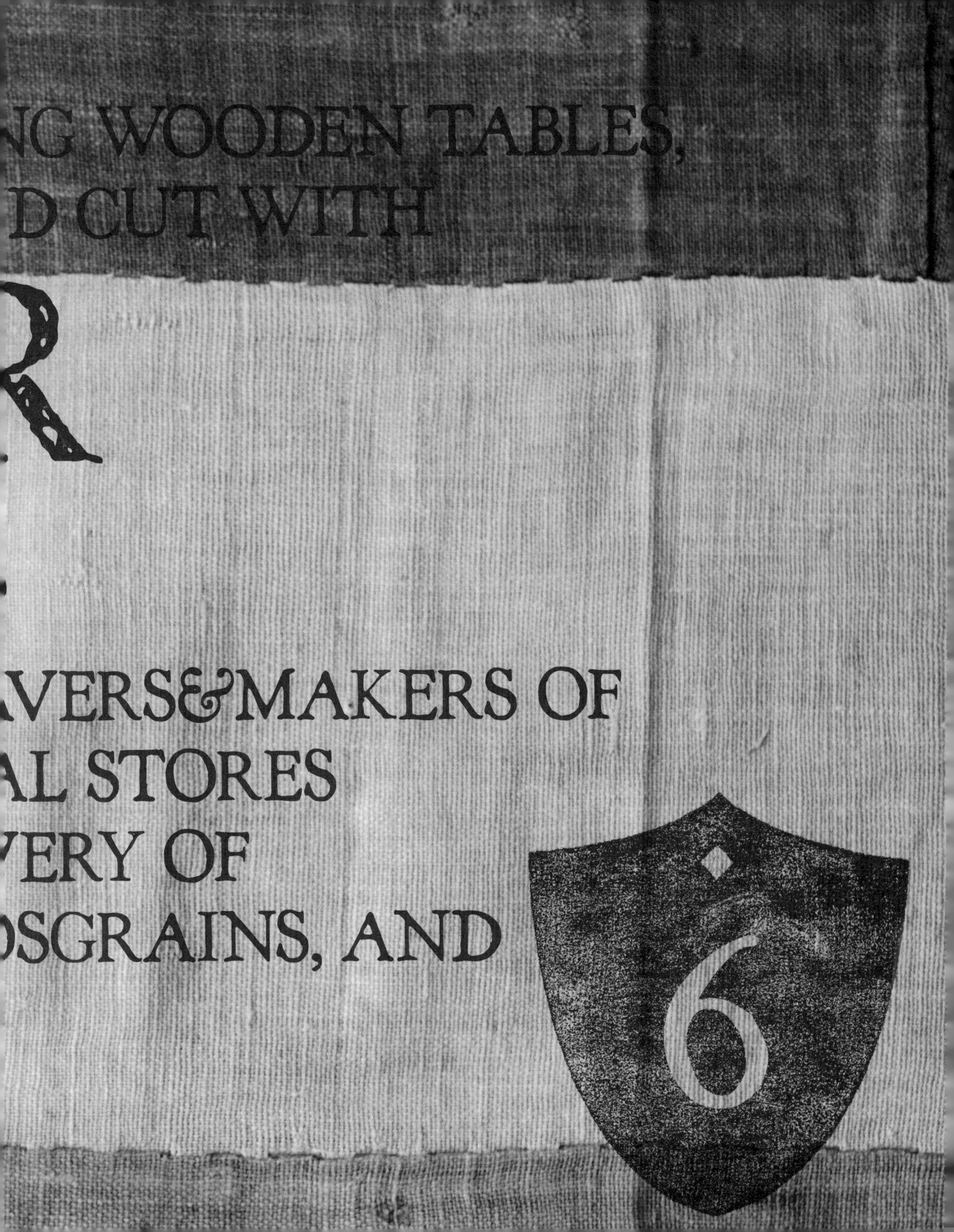

NG WOODEN TABLES,
D CUT WITH

R

VERS&MAKERS OF
AL STORES
VERY OF
OSGRAINS, AND

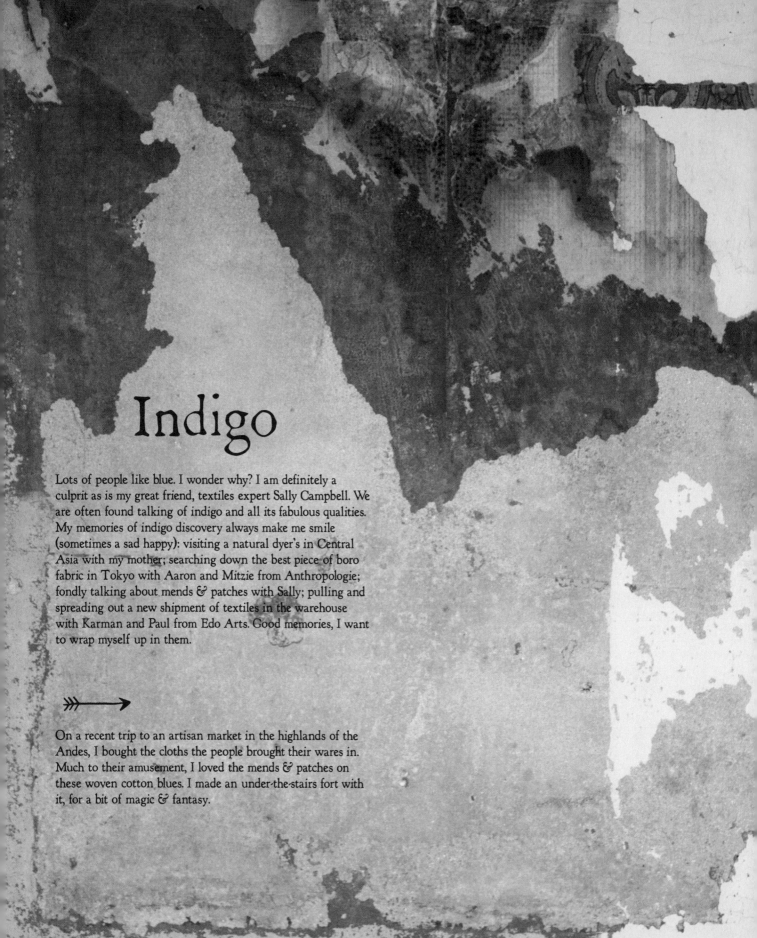

Indigo

Lots of people like blue. I wonder why? I am definitely a culprit as is my great friend, textiles expert Sally Campbell. We are often found talking of indigo and all its fabulous qualities. My memories of indigo discovery always make me smile (sometimes a sad happy): visiting a natural dyer's in Central Asia with my mother; searching down the best piece of boro fabric in Tokyo with Aaron and Mitzie from Anthropologie; fondly talking about mends & patches with Sally; pulling and spreading out a new shipment of textiles in the warehouse with Karman and Paul from Edo Arts. Good memories, I want to wrap myself up in them.

On a recent trip to an artisan market in the highlands of the Andes, I bought the cloths the people brought their wares in. Much to their amusement, I loved the mends & patches on these woven cotton blues. I made an under-the-stairs fort with it, for a bit of magic & fantasy.

APARTMENT
FOR RENT

Layer your bed with blues. Here a vintage futon cover, French ticking, and Belgian flour sack sit together under a photograph of Japanese workman's shoes. All shades of indigo blues.

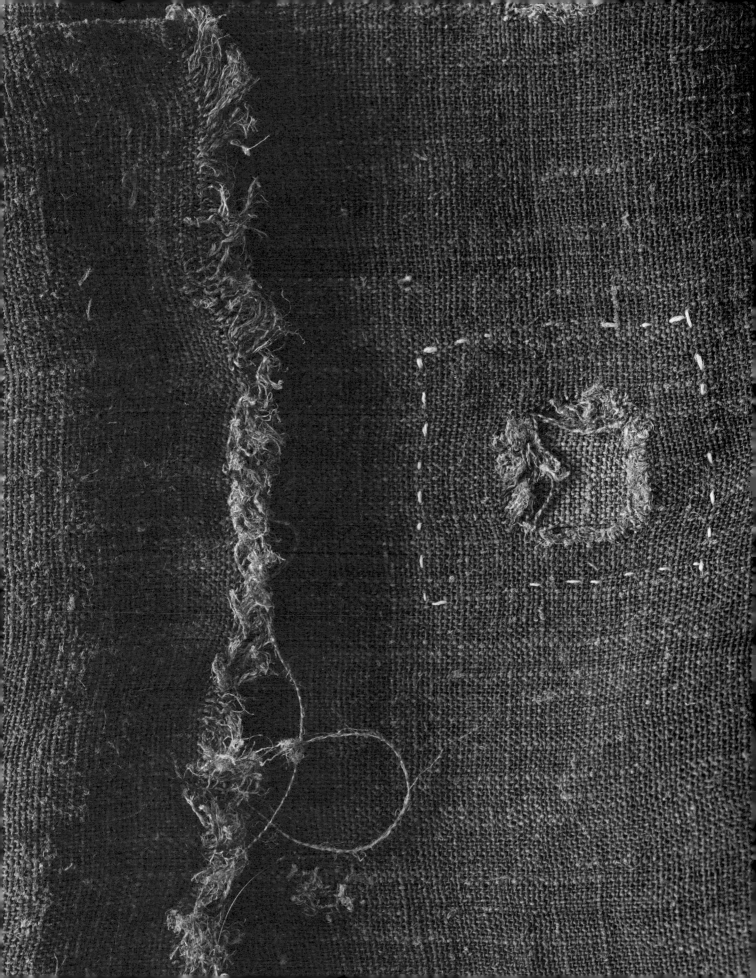

Linen
&homespun

It's crunchy, textured, absorbent, durable, loomed, natural, and thick (well, usually). I like to surround myself with it in every room: bath, kitchen, bedroom. In my time, I have found a couple of old rolls and felt over-the-moon excited. I sleep on linen sheets I bought in a backstreet *brocante* when my friend Edwina was getting married in a barn outside Bordeaux. Ah, living the dream and listening to rural French on the radio. One of my top five places to visit is a linen company that manufactures old-fashioned towels, sheets, cloths, etc. in Transylvania (where I'll find my own Dracula, of course).
I made my drapes at The Society inc. simply by cutting lengths, sewing on old brass curtain rings, and using a kilt pin as a tie back – gorgeous.

Embrace the dustcover look of a locked-up mansion. If your vintage linen doesn't cover the whole sofa, layer in patches and continue to add tone and texture with the cushions. These are old French sheets and Belgian flour sacks. Let the covers fall to the floor – linen has such a body-filled drape.

[PREVIOUS PAGE]
This all-important stack of linen travels to all my jobs. I use it for upholstery, color, & texture reference.

Milliners' notions

When I was living in NYC, I thought I knew every shop there was to know until I accidentally stumbled upon Dulken & Derrick, one of the few manufacturers of handmade fabric flowers. Ones like the signature camellia of Chanel and even Carrie Bradshaw's numbers. Brown-labeled boxes line all the walls & shelves, many with Chanel, Carolina Herrera, Oscar de la Renta, Alexander McQueen, and the like scrawled across the front.
I was passed a velvet-lined tray and left to roam into the depths. That day I was into dusty pinks and gray browns (thinking of silk stockings and chemises). I spent a small fortune but have never forgotten my first visit.

Fabric flowers laid out ready to adorn a present or wear in my hair.

Stack & lean empty frames against the wall. Use as the base for your display of vintage notions. Attach with tape or simply rest or tuck your pieces into the frame work.

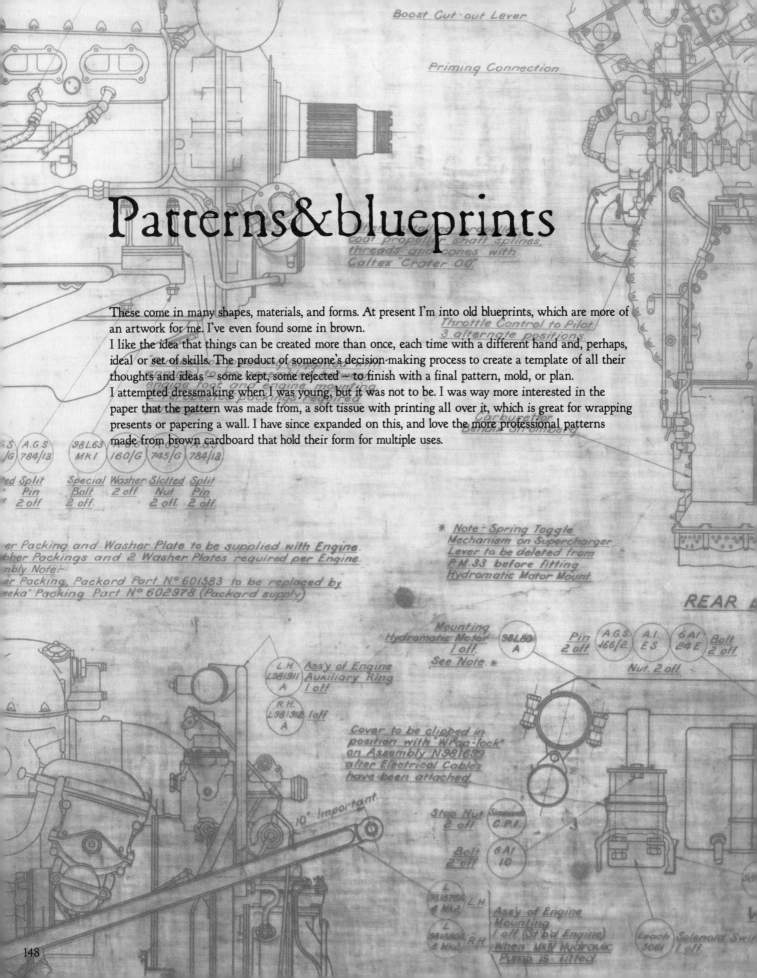

Patterns&blueprints

These come in many shapes, materials, and forms. At present I'm into old blueprints, which are more of an artwork for me. I've even found some in brown.

I like the idea that things can be created more than once, each time with a different hand and, perhaps, ideal or set of skills. The product of someone's decision-making process to create a template of all their thoughts and ideas – some kept, some rejected – to finish with a final pattern, mold, or plan.

I attempted dressmaking when I was young, but it was not to be. I was way more interested in the paper that the pattern was made from, a soft tissue with printing all over it, which is great for wrapping presents or papering a wall. I have since expanded on this, and love the more professional patterns made from brown cardboard that hold their form for multiple uses.

An old lamp found at auction gets a new life. I painted the shade in white and attached some pattern paper with pegs. When on, the light shines beautifully through the paper.

Under a bank of louvered shutters, a bundle of old blueprints becomes wallpaper. They make for an interesting backdrop, steeped in history.

ENGINEERS' HAMMERS

BALL PANE

STRAIGHT PANE

CROSS PANE

SQUARE SLEDGE

LEAD HAMMER

Ribbons

Ribbons were one of my first
collections and I have never grown
out of them. Although I do not sport
them in my pigtails anymore, I use
them for color inspiration, making
a package special, tying a placecard
on a napkin, or have them simply
because they're beautiful.

My ribbons are now housed in yellow
vintage labeled shoeboxes, each color
in a different box, all special, and all
treasured. My mother used to buy me
two lengths of ribbon, each a yard
long, so I would always have one for
each pigtail. I continue to buy two
yards at a time, a leftover habit from
childhood, but have no need to cut
the length in half these days.

Velvet embellished ribbon lengths
are easily tacked over a doorway.
What a lovely entrance to a room or
a beautiful visual as you peer down a
hallway, with ribbons catching in
the breeze.

Safety pins

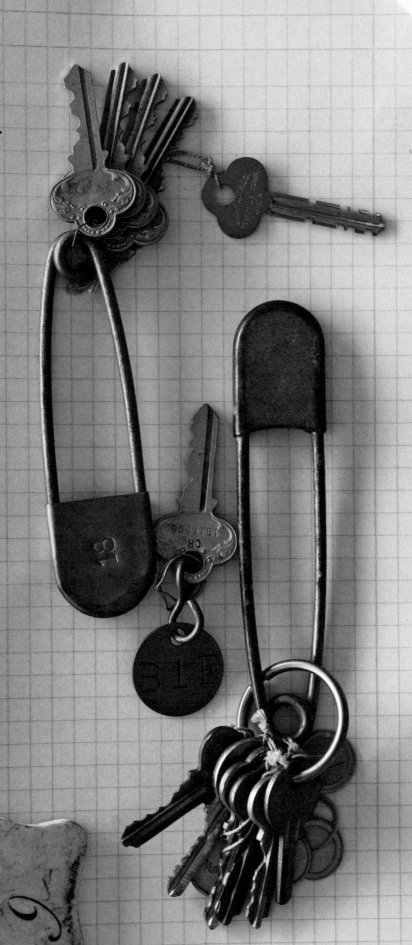

Ah, the variety. Like pushpins, safety pins come in many shapes & forms depending on the country of origin and the purpose. The Japanese version of the kilt pin is a favorite at present, fine and in a gold finish. For my hardware range, I have just designed some based on the oversize laundry bag pins of the past and oversize fine kilt pins. A great invention that is both functional and beautiful.

As I do in my shop, use an oversize kilt pin as a tie back for your linen drapes. Make sense of all your keys, and use as a key ring.

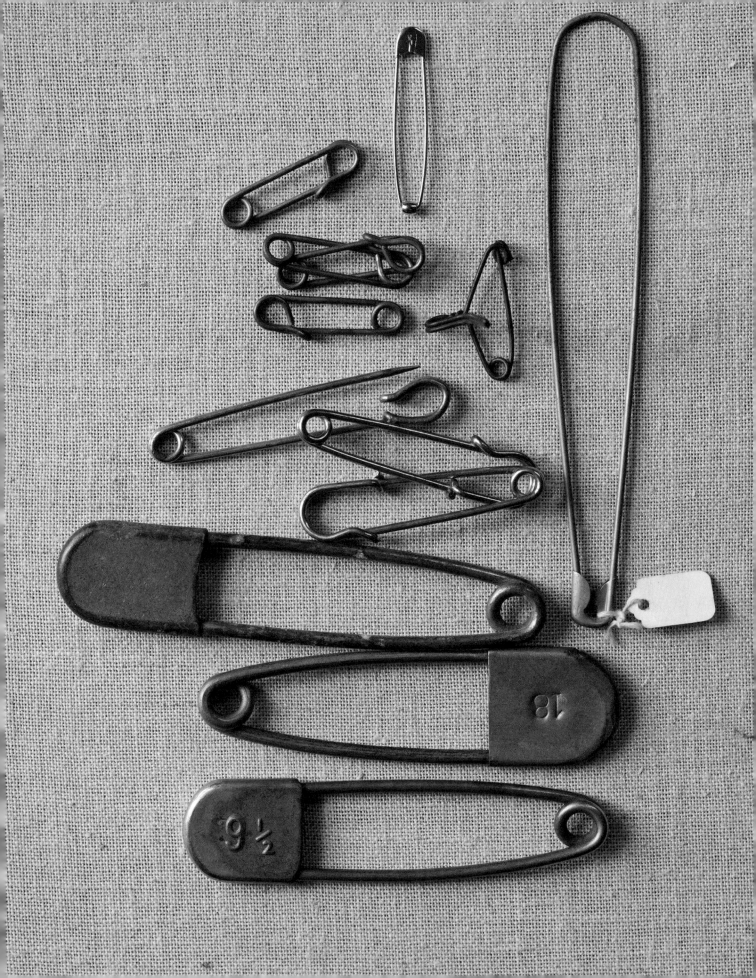

PAPER FOR A PURPOSE;
THE INCIDENTALS MADE

EPHEM

OFTEN OVERLOOKED OR
MARKS FROM BEING MAN
TIMES THUMBED

OM IT,

ERA

CARDED; WITH

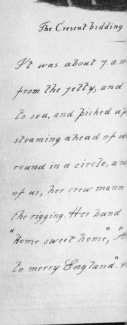

paroquets of every shade colour and discription. Also cockatoo's in large numbers, besides quite a host of smaller birds, We also had a pair of laughing jackasses and a sort of white kywi. In the animal line was a fawn &

SHIPS PETS

Diferent Races of People met with During the Tour.

MALTESE LADY

ARAB

MALAY

AUSTRALIAN ABORIGINAL

WEST AFRICAN

AMERICAN INDIAN

we where met
" who took over
he "Terpeschore"

The Cresent bidding

It was about 7. a.m
from the jetty, and
to sea, and picked up
steaming ahead of us
round in a circle, an
of us, her crew mann
the rigging. Her band
"Home sweet home", A
to merry England." I

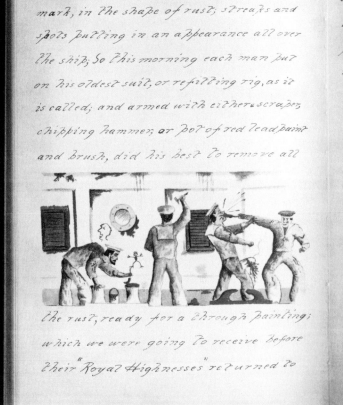

mark, in the shape of rust; streaks and spots putting in an appearance all over the ship; So this morning each man put on his oldest suit, or refitting rig, as it is called; and armed with either a scraper, chipping hammer, or pot of red lead paint and brush, did his best to remove all the rust, ready for a through painting; which we were going to receive before their "Royal Highnesses" returned to

turned to proceed on board, the cheering was deffening

Atlases, maps, &dictionaries

I like to think of myself as a globetrotter, treasure-seeker,
& explorer, and to be those things I need atlases, maps, and
dictionaries from other countries. I actively seek these out in
flea and antique markets while traveling, and love to find ones
in other languages or so very out of date that you can see how
countries' boundaries & borders have changed over time.
I have a stack of linen-covered dictionaries: Icelandic to
English, Russian to English, etc. I appreciate the different texts
and sounds, and even the straight columns appeal to me.

[PREVIOUS PAGE]
A map/journal I found at a second-hand
book store is color photocopied and
tacked on the wall. This could be done
for a celebration or because you like it,
semi-permanent or just for the day.

⋙⟶

Framed maps create a backdrop for a
bed. Find places that are important to
you, enlarge, copy, and display.

[NEXT PAGE]
A Russian dictionary, blown up and
attached as wall paper, creates an
inviting entrance.

nr book is plainly enough written to be
understood by those who peruse it with atten...
...indifferency, or else I have writ mine so ob...
...al it is in vain to go about to mend it. Locke
...ver go about, as in former times, to hide n...
...their vices; but expose them freely to view. Swift

aside. To err; to deviate from th...
man's wife go aside, and commit a trespass...
...him. Numbers 5
o between. To interpose; to mo...
etween two.
...e between them, as I said; but more than...
...loved her; for, indeed, he was mad for lo...
Shakspeare.
by. To pass away unnoticed.
...ou come my tardiness to chide,
...in time and passion, lets go by
...ast acting of your dread command?
Shakspeare's Henry...
...he more our carver's excellent,
...o by some sixteen years, and makes her...
...now. Shakspeare's Winter's Tale.
...to us? The time goes by; away. Shaks
...y. To find or get in the condi...
...t with men a woman ever
...orse, whatever be her cause. Hu...
...o go by the worst that contends wi...
...t is too mighty for him. L'Estrange
To observe as a rule.
...e supposed, that by searching out t...
...of the size and form of a stone; u...
...uency of the fits, and violence of th...
...a better rule to go by. Sharp's Surgery
...n. To be swallowed; to b...
...not rejected.
...idiculous, nothing so impossible, bu...
...ole with him for truth and earnest.
L'Estrange
...asily go down in its own natural for...
...udges. Dryden
...y, bread will go down. Locke
...o wise to leave their proceedings to...
...by reasoners at a distance, who of...
...into the systems that do not only go...
...in the coffeehouse, but are supplies...
...the present age. Swift
...out. To do the business of
...reserve thy going out and thy
Psalm
To be at liberty.
...out, and find pasture. John x. 9.
...die; to go out of life; to
...we miss were safe arrived:
...d yet, by these I see
...is cheaply bought. Shakspeare.
...ent off, not like a man that de...
...one that returned to his abode.
Tatler.
depart from a post.
...charge from you to stand,
...hey hear you speak.
Shakspeare's Henry IV.
...nake attack.
...egus,
...rn'd into his poison,
...g, as he would
Ben Jonson.
...proceed.
...war to keep that peace, but was
Sidney.
...tory.
...nly that the work of God and reli...
...pleased with it, whoever is th
Taylor.

The morning, as mistaken, turns about;
And all her early fires again *go out*. *Dryden's Auren.*
Let the acquaintance be decently buried, and the
flame rather *go out* than be smothered. *Collier.*
My blood runs cold, my heart forgets to heave,
And life itself *goes out* at thy displeasure. *Add. Cato.*
And at her felt approach and secret might,
Art after art *goes out*, and all is night. *Pope's Dunc.*

67. *To go through.* To perform thoroughly;
to execute.
Finding Pyrocl... to *go through* with
that kind of l... for his sake as
for his own t... *Sidney.*
If you can a... the statute laws
of that land... not lost all your
time there. *Spenser.*
Kings ought n... il to *go through*
with resolution... it depended on
them, but take the... their own hands.
Bacon.
He much feared the... ntrim had not steadi-
ness of mind enough to g...ough with such an un-
dertaking. *Clarendon.*
The amazing difficulty a... greatness of his account
will rather terrify than info... him, and keep him from
setting heartily about such... task, as he despairs ever
to *go through* with it. *South's Sermons.*
The powers in Germany... re borrowing money, in
order to *go through* their pa...of the expence.
Addison on the War.

68. *To go through.* To su...er; to undergo.
I tell thee that it is abs...utely necessary for the
common good that thou sh...uldest *go through* this
operation. *Arbuthnot.*

69. *To go upon.* To tak... as a principle.
This supposition I have...one *upon* through those
papers. *Addison.*

70. The senses of this word are very indis-
tinct; its general not...on is motion or pro-
gression. It common...y expresses passage
from a place, in opposit...on to *come*. This
is often obse...ble even in figurative ex-
pressions. ...say the words that *go* before and th...ne after; to-day *goes* away
and to-mo...omes.

Go to. *interj.* ...e, come, take the right
course. A...ful exhortation.
Go to then,...ar renowned son
Of great Ap...thy famous might
In medicin... *Spenser.*
Go to, g...art a foolish fellow;
Let me b...th...*Shakspeare's Twelfth Night.*
My fa...bought with words like these:
Go to;...your tongue another tale. *Rowe.*

Go-by. ...Delusion; artifice; circum-
ven...er-reach.
...pr...apprentice is instructed how to adulte-
ra...rnish, and give you the *go by* upon occa-
si...raster may be charged with neglect.
Collier on Pride.

Go...r. *n. s.* [*go* and *cart*.] A machine in
w...children are inclosed to teach them
to...lk, and which they push forward
wi...ut danger of falling.
Young children, who are try'd in
Go-cart...to keep their steps from sliding,
When members knit, and legs grow stronger,
Make use of such machine no longer. *Prior.*

Goad. *n. s.* [ʒað, Sax.] A pointed instru-
ment with which oxen are driven forward.
Oft in his harden'd hand a *goad* he bears. *Pope.*

To **Goad.** *v. a.* [from the noun.]
1. To prick or drive with the goad.
2. To incite; to stimulate; to instigate; to
drive forward.
Most dangerous
Is that temptation, that doth *goad* us on
To sin in loving virtue. *Shaks. Measure for Measure.*

Gall of *goat*, and slips of...
We Cyclops care not for...
Nor other blest ones, we a...
You may draw naked bo...
their paper mills, upon go...
The little bear that rock'...
The swan, whose borrow'd...
Are grac'd with light; the...
With heav'n, and duty rais...
GOATBEARD. *n. s.* [g...
capri.] A plant.
GOATCHAFER. *n. s.* ...
beetle.
GOATHERD. *n. s.* [ʒa...
feeder or tender.]...
ment is to tend goat...
Is not thilk same *goo*...
That sits on yonder ba...
Whose straying herd...
Among the bushes ran...
They first gave the *goat*...
the marquis and his serva...
stack.
GOATMARJORAM. *n....*
GOATBEARD.
GOATSMILK. *n. s.* [go...
more properly two w...
After the fever and such...
ed, asses and *goatsmilk* ma...
GOATMILKER. *n. s.* [go...
of owl so called from...
GOAT'S *Rue.* *n. s.* [gale...
Goat's Rue has the reput...
pharmick and sudorifick;...
boiled; with us it is of no...
GOATSKIN. *n. s.* [goat...
Then fill'd two *goatskins*...
With water one, and one w...
GOATS-THORN. *n. s.* [go...
GOATISH. *adj.* [from...
goat in any quality:...
An admirable evasion o...
lay his *goatish* disposition...

The last is notorious for...
not unlike the beard of tha...

GOB. *n. s.* [gobe, Fr.]...
low word.
Do'st think I have so lit...
a *gob* of money?
GOBBET. *n. s.* [gobe,...
much as can be swa...
Therewith she spew'd o...
A flood of poison, horrible...
Full of great lumps of fles...
By devilish policy art th...
And, like ambitious Sylla...
With *gobbets* of thy mothe...
The cooks, slicing it int...
a prong of iron, and hang...
The giant gorg'd with fl...
Lay stretch'd at length, an...
Belching raw *gobbets* fro...
With purple wine and cru...
To **GOBBET.** *v. a.* [f...
swallow at a mouth...
Down comes a kite pow...
bets up both together.
To **GOBBLE.** *v. a.* [...
Fr.] To swallow ha...
noise.
The sheep were so keen...
gobbled up now and the...
with them.
Of last year's corn i...

shop

sh

Cards: flash, playing, &others

I discovered an oversize bundle of cards displaying nursery rhymes in a flea market in Sandwich, Illinois. I have since picked them up throughout the States. They are two-sided and often have typed running writing on the back. Featuring the same word in regular type on the front (or vice versa), these teaching tools translate so easily into your interior styling as wall art. Or have them casually leaning on your stairs to read as you wander up & down, or put them anywhere else you choose. So perfectly die-cut on each corner and often the loveliest shade of aged paper. I like to mix up words, numbers, phrases, or letters in unusual combinations, or just have one on its own.

My very good friend James Merrell and I find cards, mostly in random places. Discarded cards are so curious and intriguing. I enjoy receiving texts from James such as "soggy jack of hearts found at Mott & Crosby," or from me "seven of spades found in windswept bush in Palm Beach." My random cards often find themselves propped up on mantelpieces or just stuck in trophies on my shelves.

Perhaps it is the many card games that my siblings & I learned from my grandmother and played constantly while we were growing up. We were very good and competitive at 500, gin rummy, canasta, and blackjack, and could play an energetic game of double patience!

fl

sp

》》》⟶

The abovementioned bundle of flash cards attached to the wall. They do not go all around but skim over the doorway and asymmetrically off to one side. Add to the display as you find more, or intersperse with other paper finds.

keep

er   er

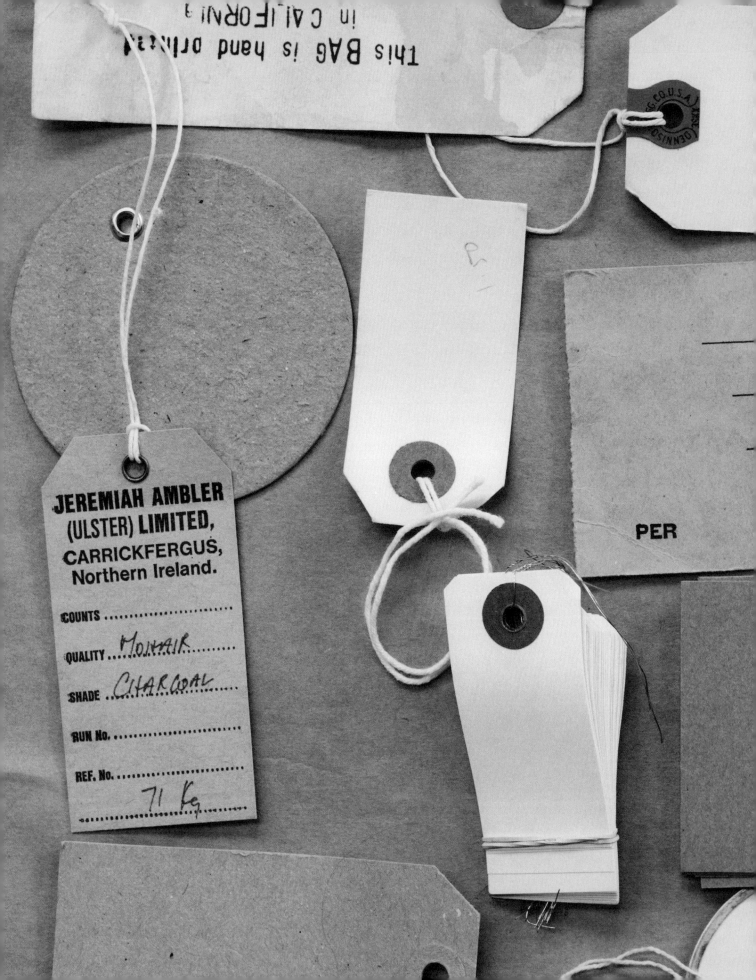

Luggage&porters' tags

S

ABANA

CE

DATE

These conjure up a time of slow travel: steamships, trunks, and
the all-important porter. The tags that would link you with
your possessions, plus the name of your destination to minimize
confusion upon arrival! I use the newer version of these daily in
my shop, and have a very extensive selection of colors, sizes, &
shapes, both new & old, that I have picked up while gallivanting
to stationery stores, flea markets, artists' suppliers, & hardware
stores. I have since made them into metal form to be used as
drawer pulls in my hardware range for Anthropologie.

This cabinet had so many drawers, it was necessary for me to label their contents so I knew where my things were!

Old packaging

During my years of styling, I developed some strange habits (or were they always there!?). I styled food shoots for many years, so was always on the lookout for unusual table props. Traveling constantly, I began picking up wrapped sugar cubes and matchbooks from various nooks & crannies. As well as these souvenirs, I grew very interested in paper food wrappings, particularly vintage ones like tapas paper with words printed on it, bonbon cones, place cards, cheese labels, paper napkins, cupcake patty pans, foil chocolate wrappers, berry containers, and amaretto papers to incorporate into my photographs.

These old barber-stripe straws transport you to a forgotten time of soda fountains and vans that delivered soda to your house. Don't be shy about adopting these into your life as a gentle reminder of your own childhood.

NIETZSCHE   THUS SPOKE ZARATHUSTRA

Books

When I was traveling from Adelaide in
South Australia due north to Darwin,
Northern Territory, on The Ghan (a
railroad named after the Afghan cameleers
who once traversed the same route), I met
a travel photographer. He told me about an
old mosaic school in Murano, Italy, that
he had recently covered, and later sent me
pictures of the glass library there. I had
the shelving replicated to my interpretation
& specification, and it now takes up walls
upstairs & downstairs at The Society inc.,
with a Putnam rolling ladder to allow for
easy access to all my books.
Books are the ultimate styling tool.
They make a space feel like a home and
are a direct reference to your interests
& fantasies, and a reflection of whose
space it is. They can create a beautiful
backdrop (as mine do) or simply add
height, color, & a point of view on
tables, shelves, and mantels.

[NEXT PAGE]
Have a sense of humor and
use recycled bricks with
favorite book titles painted
on, for display and as
bookends.

Wall [papers]

Ahhh, the luxury & fun of building sets on someone else's budgets. Although this is a past dream, owning and loving wallpaper is not. I have bought so many beautiful rolls of wallpaper for both work & pleasure, and one of my one-stop shops is Secondhand Rose in NYC. Not only can you invigorate and define a space with times-gone-past but also just use it for color & pattern inspiration.

Wall paper does not always have to be in the form of traditional wallpaper – do not dismiss old books, newspapers, pianola scrolls, paper patterns, or even squares of colored paper to paste up and make your own.

EVERYDAY MATERIALS TR
FOR CENTURIES; NATURAL
TRANSLATED&MANIPULAT
PUT TO FUNCTIONAL USE
HONES
&HUM

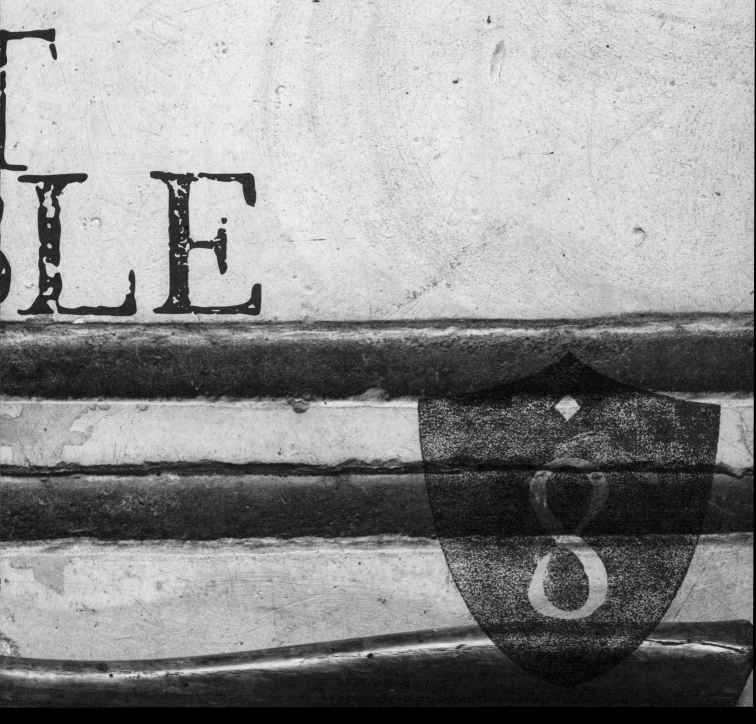

Blackboard&slate

I believe I was born in the wrong era, although I do love the liberation of technology! Ah, the romance of the time when you walked to school and had your very own slate to write the day's work on. I have collected some of the smaller slates bound in leather and wood, and one even has a name etched into it.

I have created a range of twelve colors of chalkboard paint so you can put a blackboard on a wall or piece of furniture any time you please, in any color you please.

[PREVIOUS PAGE]
I picked up this ancient crumbly roof tile from an abandoned barn south of Dublin when I was on a shoot for an American magazine. I used the original holes in the slate to attach it over the top of some pretty average kitchen tiles and now use for Smith's Lake Nan's pancakes recipe which are really crepes!

Candles

Candlelight adds a warming ambient element to any room, whether the candles are scented or not. I have candles of all shapes & sizes: church tapers, beeswax, birthday cake, elaborate hand-molded & embellished Mexican ones, figures, wedding cake toppers, and the rest.

Attach tapers to a table with their own wax for a romantic centerpiece. At dusk, light them and let them pool on the table as the dinner party starts.

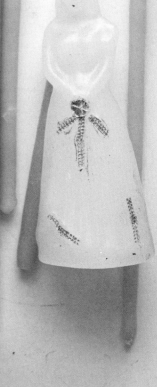

Handblown glass

Years ago I found a market outside of Paris, a *jambon & brocante* market to be exact. It was the best market I have ever been to, not just for the fabulous finds, but for the fact that at lunchtime the stalls closed, and store owners pulled out their beautiful short-stemmed vintage glasses, linen napkins, & silver cutlery to accompany their just as fabulous cheeses, oysters, & ham (of course!). It was such a simple daily ritual that I have now incorporated it into my life, and love nothing more than sipping my Pouilly-Fuissé from one of these glasses.

I have collected them from around the world (not just France) and embrace their mix & match quality, and the stories & memories their purchase holds.

Western Sycamore
(Platanus racemosa)

California Bay
(Umbellularia californica)

Porcelain

My paper obsession saw a new outlet when I began to collect porcelain versions of classic-shaped paper vessels. A strawberry basket, paper plate, hot chip container, espresso cup: I love that something usually tossed away after one use suddenly has a longer life, by being made of something precious. I first saw this approach by an Australian artist, Nicole Lister. After buying her cups, I found other curious pieces in NYC, London, & Paris. I stick to white, and let the pieces speak for themselves in their simplicity. I like the surprise element of the traditionally disposable becoming permanent.

A loose grouping of related objects – leaf ceramics, a medicinal bottle filled with giant seeds, a box of porcelain leaves, leaf specimens, and a sprig of faux fir – makes for an interesting and very unscientific mantel display.

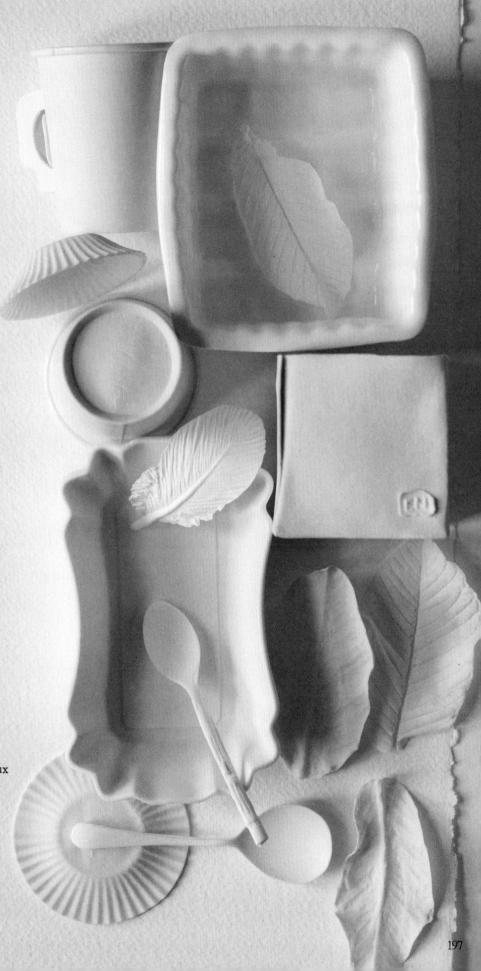

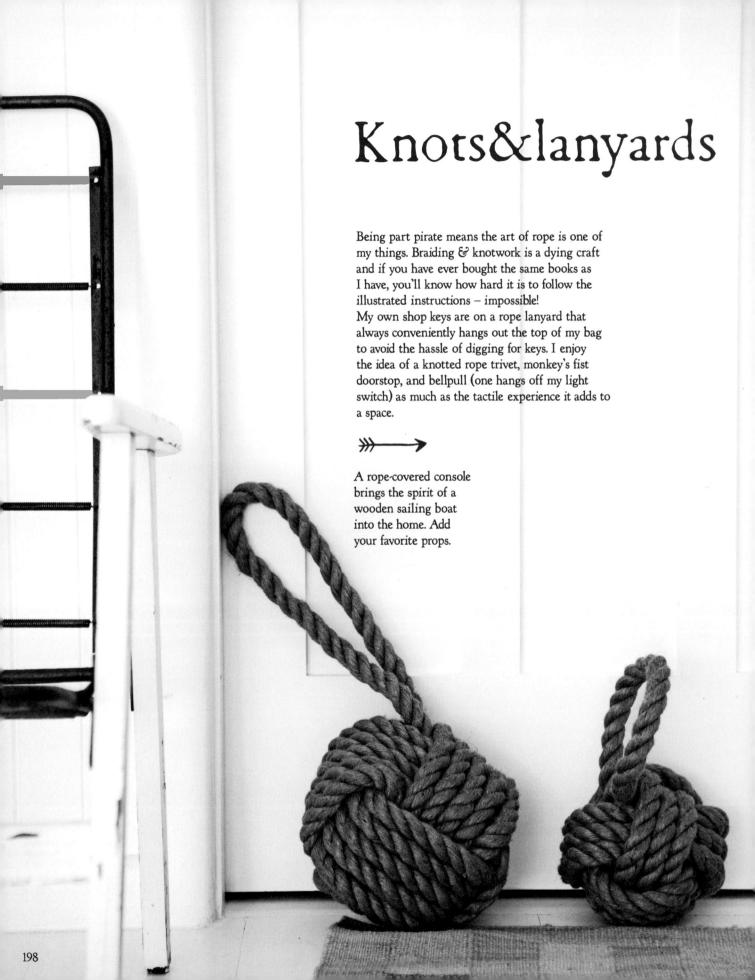

Knots&lanyards

Being part pirate means the art of rope is one of my things. Braiding & knotwork is a dying craft and if you have ever bought the same books as I have, you'll know how hard it is to follow the illustrated instructions – impossible!
My own shop keys are on a rope lanyard that always conveniently hangs out the top of my bag to avoid the hassle of digging for keys. I enjoy the idea of a knotted rope trivet, monkey's fist doorstop, and bellpull (one hangs off my light switch) as much as the tactile experience it adds to a space.

A rope-covered console brings the spirit of a wooden sailing boat into the home. Add your favorite props.

In the commercial interiors I design, you can often see my stamp through the entanglement of rope hanging through beams and holding up mirrors. In my shop, props swing through the space, ships sail from the banisters, and you may even come across a couch hanging mid-air.

If you can, it looks beautiful to splice a rope. However, if this is beyond your capabilities, a double granny will always suffice. Try these for fun:
Figure-of-eight
Monkey's fist
Lover's knot
Turk's-head
Tom fools
The Butterfly
Note: See *The Ashley Book of Knots* for instruction.

In Galapagos, I visited an old stone stacked house, now a restaurant, that was surrounded by water. We arrived by boat and, as we touched down, were greeted with these simple coils of ropes as mats. Genius! This was originally the home of Gus Angermeyer, one of the first explorers from faraway shores to settle in the Galapagos Islands. He built his home from natural resources: lava, rocks, & wood and was famous for reading Shakespeare & Einstein, and sharing his adventures with a lucky few.

Choose like-minded accessories that can hang. Here, a knotted rope shopping bag, and a lanyard with whistle on the ready for when you jump on an awaiting boat.

Vessels

It appears I just cannot get enough of slightly askew handmade, often hand-thrown plates, bowls, cups, and other vessels in natural colors. On return from my travels, my luggage always contains at least one new vessel. It is more often than not made by a local artist, in an indigenous material: wood, bone, clay, stone, wire, vine, glass, shell. They're for everyday use.

A vintage water decanter, left over from long luxurious train travel, gets a new life as a container for bath oil.

[PREVIOUS PAGE]
A seasonal table set with just picked cabbages and a variety of vessels: glazed porcelain teacups from Vietnam, a classic white jug, and handwoven hemp bags add adventure, texture, & scale to your tablescape.

THE STRANGE & WONDERF

ODDITI

& CURI

THAT FIT INTO LIFE IN TH
UNCONVENTIONAL OF W

BITS&BOBS

ES

OSITIES

MOST MAGICAL AND

9

A vintage German porcelain doll stands to the wall as if in disgrace. A detail in a larger picture that demands a closer look.

I borrowed (and never returned) some framed Indian doll heads from my parents many years ago. I enjoyed it that people either loved them or hated them (yes, a strong word, but true). Since then, I have sought out various random body parts from flea markets and junk shops.

There are two shops in San Francisco and one in NYC that have fueled my curiosity for oddities over the years: Tail of the Yak, Paxton Gate and Obscura. I'm not sure if I have always liked unattached doll parts, fake eyes, teeth sewn on cards, etc., but maybe I have. These things are often small, and for those who notice, cause a double take.

Limbs&body parts

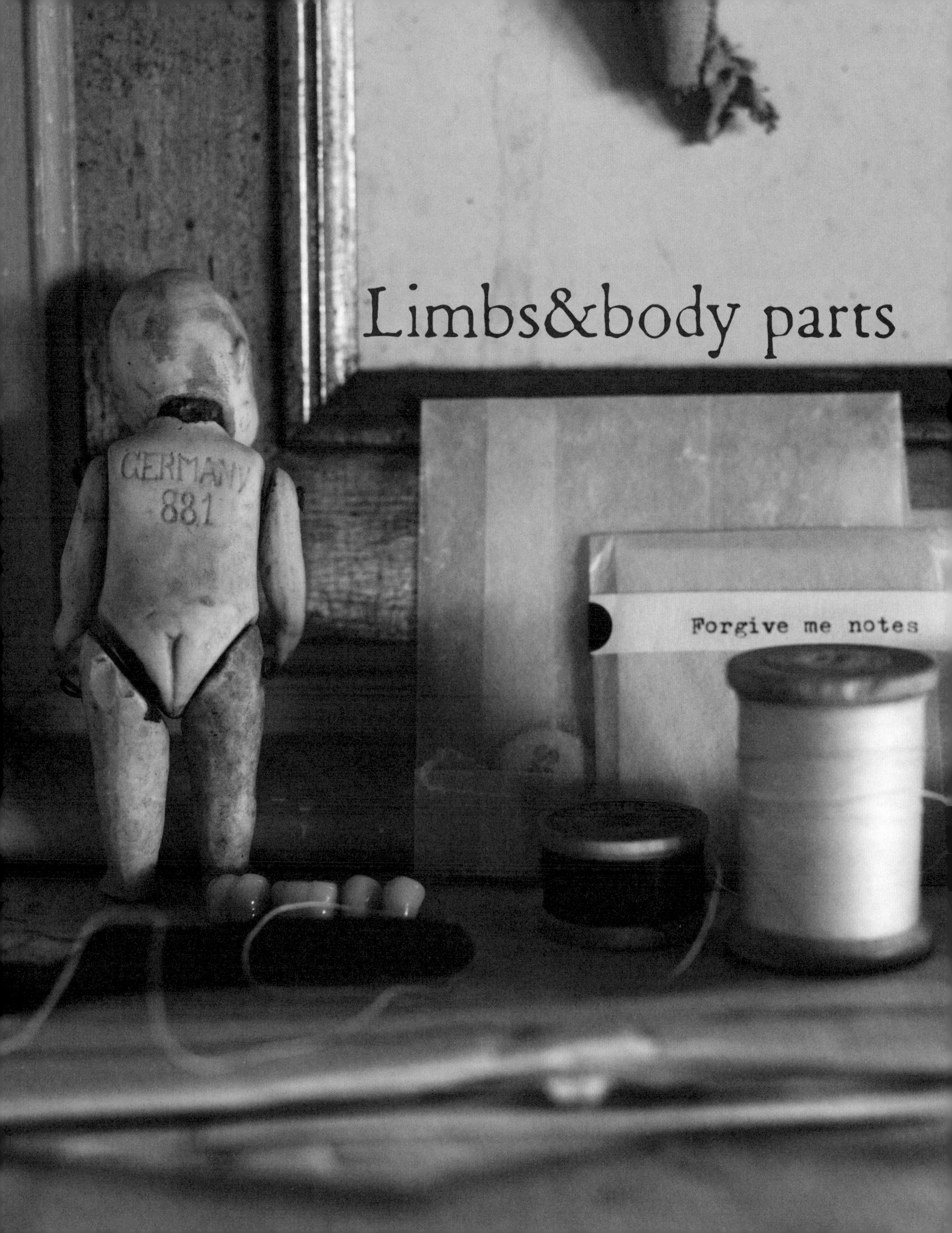

GERMANY
88.1

Forgive me notes

In some instances it will be found more convenient to use adhesive plaster to hold wounds together than to sew them together. When adhesive plaster is to be applied, wash the wound, as already described, wipe the edges dry, and then hold the wound together and apply the adhesive plaster first so as to hold the central part of the wound together. Then other strips may be so applied as to hold the extremities of the wound together. The strips should have intervals of from a fourth to a half inch between them. The width of the strips of adhesive plaster may vary from a fourth of an inch to one inch in width not entirely encircle a limb, lest they arrest the should be sufficiently long to take good hold either side of a wou together. between the strips the secretic to escape. Should betw the discharges fron and pain, and delay h been stitched together, it is often desirable to apr plaster, so as to keep the wounded su tion. The dressings whi the cloths wet in wat applied over the plaster and whi has been simply stitched together

When nd has been dress placed at perfect rest, in an ele check all bleeding, and a one which is left Besid

ing es exceedingly. larg e from a wound, so tha are a change may be necessary th wound y also be necessar since ca c I n d the wou

My dad has had a mustache forever. Maybe that's where my fascination with them came from, or was it our next-door neighbor, the conductor, who had a white ringmaster one that needed to be waxed. When I travel I look for mustached men in photographs & paintings, plus I recently started stocking mugs with mustaches and even named one of my paints "Mustache."

Mustached men

found outside Moooi, Amsterdam
whilst on bicycles in the rain
with Mckie & Tamara, October 20

Shields

The icon for my shop is a shield based on an old enamel school badge, similar to the one I used to wear. I have always admired the shape of shields and now that it is so synonymous with my brand, I use them liberally in interiors and logos I design, and even the jewelry I wear.

On the day I bought my shop, I found a rose gold shield ring, large in size and perfect for my thumb. I wear it to this day and it reminds me of the joy & accomplishment I felt in starting The Society inc. You may have a favorite icon that can be used in the same way.

Although traditionally made of metal, this shield is cut from denim, embroidered, & appliquéd to ticking. It adds textures & layers to a plain linen sofa, as well as recording your personal stories and important dates.

STOP TALKING

THE SOCIETY INC

18 STEWART STREET
PADDINGTON NSW 2021
AUSTRALIA

WWW.THESOCIETYINC.COM.AU
TEL: +612 93311592

HB

Strange little paintings

I visited the isolated Nukus Museum of Art, Uzbekistan, with my mother. All these amazing Russian avant-garde artists whose works were banned by Stalin are on show in this incredible museum. Outside, there was a small exhibition of local children's art. I bought a drawing of a blackbird. On a recent trip to Amsterdam, while visiting Moooi's HQ, I picked up a discarded portrait with a green background and strapped it to the back of my bicycle. It now sits comfortably in my annex with other such finds.

I like picking up flat things when traveling, and paintings fit this requirement, especially when small. Although I randomly collect paintings without a specific subject matter, it's more about the place & trip for me; you could pick a theme and run with it, for example, portraits, landscapes, or trees.

I met Lesley of Swarm at her house, and she gave me this bag made from a painting. A useful bag, and a beautiful prop to be left out and admired.

I often like to use what's available – a hook not quite in the right place is perfect for these paintings. Don't worry about them not matching in subject, height, or color; here, anything goes.

Typography
&the written word

Alphabet letters constantly pop up in my interiors, whether it's a giant letter suspended
behind a bed, a wood cutout painted and spelling out a word, or even a tiny lettered
ceramic box that sits so innocently on a console, big enough for only a pair of diamond
earrings or a tooth. For my commercial interiors and around the shop, I have a fabulous
signwriter who tolerates my quest for the perfect font (I often have a new favorite). Most
recently I had him write on the walls of a bar in Shipley. The more handwritten, stamped,
silkscreened, or irregular & inconsistent the better.

Not only do objects assist me with inspiration for color palettes, the written word also has
a huge influence. I am a big reader of history, pictures, stories, poetry, & point form. Often
a word or phrase speaks to me in color and then gets translated into a palette, or it can
remain in its true form and get integrated into my interiors. I never shy away from writing
favorite quotes on walls or floors or even myself in pencil, tattoo, or signwriting.

How Not to get that

<u>A success article.</u>

Mr. Harkins, the president
organization or other short — (w
who
hand and looked me fearlessly in th
I felt, going to like Mr. Harki as an

"Sit down," he suggested
suggested, enthusiastically, that
I did so, and He had We discu
apt.
        , and education. We wen
lunch and discussed education
time. I thought I had folly I'd better that I w
        studied doubt paining.

MAGIC & LUCK

THE UNEXPECTED FUN & F
OLD-FASHIONED SIDESHOW
FUNHOUSES; THOUGHTS O
& PRACTICAL JOKES, AND
MIXED SWEETS

TRICKS,
Y DIPS,

NTASY OF
FAIRS, AND
TOMFOOLERY
GS OF

Amulets &talismans

Most cultures incorporate a dose of superstition into their daily lives, including a need for protection against the ever-present evil eye. I most certainly believe this, and am not often found without my amulets around my neck. For a while I flirted with antique Chinese children's clothes and although I did not pursue this collection, I love the idea that if you dressed a child up in clothes that looked and smelled of animals (such as ears on hats and tiger shoes with animal fur hidden within), the evil spirits would confuse it for an animal, and leave it to live a long, happy, & prosperous life.

Sew your amuletic bits & bobs on the inside of your clothes (and of those you love) to protect you all from evil deeds.

I love to seek out shrines both public & private, amulets that hover subtly above a shop doorway or even hang from the grille of a truck!

When wandering through daily markets, you can squirrel out the stall that sells all you need to get you through the day, often sandwiched between the fish stand and spring herb seller. Be sure to look for tigers' and wolves' teeth, stones, coins, kohl, needles, deities, small charms and beads, dried chillies, porcupine quills, honeycomb, and cloves among other magical protectors, depending on where you are in the world.

A string of bone beads that I picked up in a Seville flea market hangs on an old wire coat hanger with a carved bone Chinese talisman my mother gave me. Place it on a nail, in pride of place or even on the back of a door. These are nice ways to display your strung things (even jewelry) and an easy way to change as regularly as you like.

Your love life will be happy and harmonious.

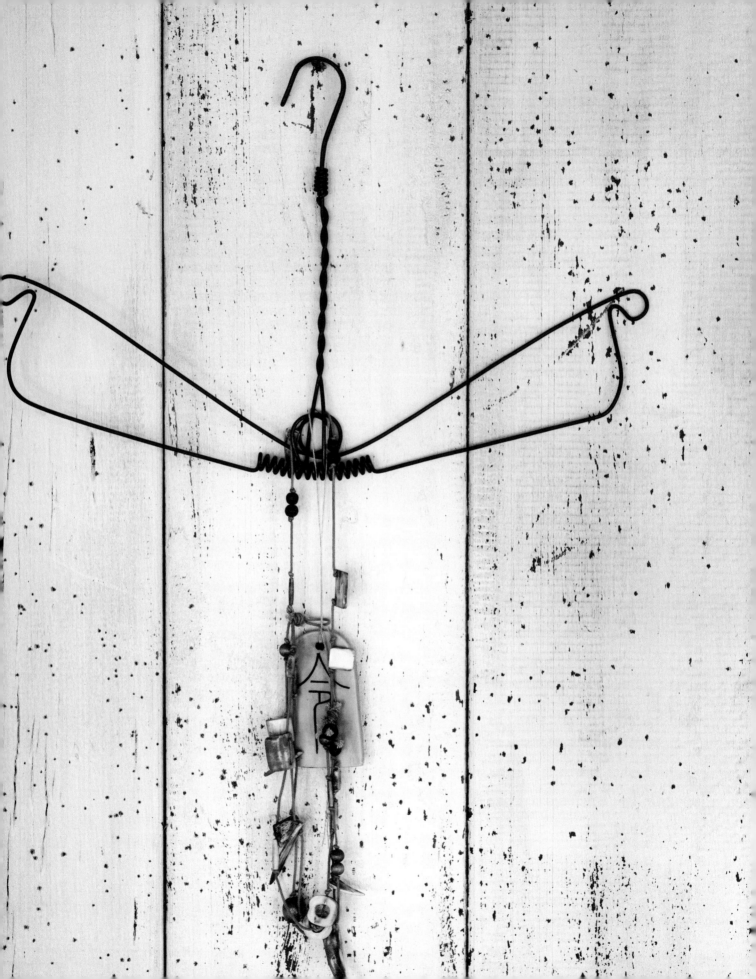

Crowns, tiaras, & masks

A paper tiara or crown of rosy thorns for me please! I have a circle of giant seaweed found at Big Sur and given to me by a past love. I'm sure a merman lost it. More pagan than regal, but glorious in its naturalness and humbleness. Not just for the human head or fancy dress, but as beautiful on a door, nail, or wall. A sparkly paper tiara can brighten up any shelf or oneself.

Picasso collected African masks for inspiration, but mine are a little different and not so uniform. I like them without rhyme, reason, or theme; old theater ones appeal to me, particularly if they are expressionless and unpainted, with the shape enough to inspire. Although, as I said, there are no rules – I am just as attracted to James Bond-esque snorkel goggles, the plastic animal shapes I buy in NYC from the novelty store, and the painted and mustached fencing mask I bought in Burton, Ohio.

A bearded man on a stick looks thoughtfully toward the light. I bought this (and others like him) from the puppetmaster in Khiva, Uzbekistan, while traveling with my mother. Accompany it with lines from a play he might star in, or keep an eye out on your travels for a leading lady.

[NEXT PAGE]
An assortment of headwear sits under a chair, part display, part in waiting to be worn for a party or performance.

Gaming paraphernalia

Over the years, I have picked up random gaming pieces (not whole sets) which come in handy when styling: a bamboo & bone mah-jongg set with dovetails, French mother of pearl round chips, plastic 1950s chess pieces, etc. I like how they feel in my hand and the different materials they are made from. I like all the strategies and deep thought they may have engendered while being gently turned during a tense game.

There is a very famous still-life by Irving Penn called *After Dinner Games* that may have sparked my desire to have gaming pieces, or perhaps it is the gambling vein that runs through the family (I am referring to an old-fashioned, slightly romantic version not that very sad & sorry variety).

Up on one of my top shelves is my great-grandmother's gambling box made of walnut. Inside is a treasure trove of cards, matchsticks (the ultimate betting device), counters, and cigarette holders. A portrait in a box.

A selection of my flat and smooth gaming pieces of various materials, casually lined up on a windowsill.

[PREVIOUS PAGE]
An afternoon to be enjoyed lakeside. Instead of the standard centerpiece selections, use an old chessboard as a trivet and scatter some of your gaming pieces among your glassware, not to use, just to look at. Your things will spark a memory, and conversation will be sprinkled with your stories.

Flags &bunting

The flags that flew – tattered through strong winds, relentless storms, high seas, and all the wildness of the ocean. The seafarer in me can't get enough of things that fly, although I am just as satisfied for my flags & bunting to live inside and/or be made of cardboard and paper.

A warning, a celebration, an indication of a win or a loss, to scare or attract attention, to signal, or even spell something out: there are so many reasons for them that they come in an endless variety of forms.

Not to be used in a formal way, I soften hard lines with flags that protrude into a space or bunting that is oh-so-casually placed over doorways & in entrances (or windows at The Society inc.).

An indoor-outdoor room, overlooking an old-school tennis court, gets ready for an afternoon of fun & games. A simple string of bunting is constructed out of cut tissue paper and encourages the sideline fans and contenders. Make it festive, make it fun.

Prizes, rosettes, &other rewards

I don't know anyone who doesn't love to win an award of some description. I haven't won enough in my life, so I have to improvise and make or buy my own. Although self-anointed, I still feel every bit the winner and suggest you follow my lead.

Make your own brown paper rosette, award yourself a gold star and stick on your forehead, purchase a porcelain trophy and felt tip your name on it, or tie a beautiful ribbon around your arm and write "You're the Best, Chuck out the Rest."

An old pirate plate rack shows off a collection of trophies, not necessarily yours. Pick them up at markets & fetes and feel like the athlete you might have been. Sprinkle with other found objects that contribute to your story.

MY LIBRARY
MUSEUMS I GET

UK

Kelvingrove Art Gallery & Museum
Argyle St
Glasgow G3 8AG
www.glasgowlife.org.uk/museums/our-museums/kelvingrove/Pages/
home.aspx/

Kew Gardens
Kew
Richmond
Surrey TW9 3AB
www.kew.org

The Museum of Everything
www.museumofeverything.com
Address changes according to exhibition. See website for details.

Natural History Museum at Tring
The Walter Rothschild building
Akeman St
Tring HP23 6AP
www.nhm.ac.uk/tring

Pitt Rivers Museum
South Parks Rd
Oxford OX1 3PP
www.prm.ox.ac.uk
Many of these smaller old school museums are the result of the lifetime's
work of one person, and become really interesting when science and
collecting merge, and the personality of the collector becomes evident.
That's the case here, where pieces are curated in item groups, such as
firelighting tools or combs, with little regard to period or time.
The overstuffed freestanding and wall cabinets, dim lighting, and
handwritten metal-edged discs and rectangular tags, holding all the data
information one might need for identification, all add to the visiting
experience and intrigue of this vision.

Sir John Soane's Museum
13 Lincoln's Inn Fields
London WC2A 3BP
www.soane.org

Snowshill Manor
Snowshill
Near Broadway WR12 7JU
www.nationaltrust.org.uk/snowshill-manor

PARIS

Cabinet of Curiosities of Bonnier de la Mosson
Muséum National d'Histoire Naturelle
57 rue Cuvier
75005 Paris
www.mnhn.fr

Hermès Museum
24 rue du Faubourg Saint-Honoré
75008 Paris
www.hermes.com
By private appointment

Musée de la Chasse et de la Nature
62 rue des Archives
75003 Paris
www.chassenature.org
This must be one of the most considered curations I have ever
experienced. It has all the things I admire in an interior: a sense of
humor, artisan-made functional pieces, custom joinery and hardware
(even the clipboards are accented with beautiful brass hardware and
illustrations), a refined color palette, attention to detail, consideration
of the vista, a mix of old & new in furniture & art, the use of superior
materials, and the interaction of a space welcoming the visitor to be an
integral part of the space and journey.
My favorite room is The Stag & Wolf Salon, with its pickled oak floors
and paneled walls, brass antler installation dagger-like on the paneled
ceiling, a huge antlered stag casually standing in the corner, tapestries
lining the walls, and two modern B&B Italia-esque blue wool, very
square sofas sitting opposite each other complete with coffee table
& floor lamps – so very residential.
It is, of course, the hunting & nature museum, and so guns & swords
are very much a part of the installation and sit comfortably beside
a menagerie of mounted animals: polar & grizzly bears, wild boars,
sleeping foxes, tigers, & lions.

Muséum National d'Histoire Naturelle
Galerie de paléontologie et d'anatomie comparée
Jardin des Plantes
2 rue Buffon
75005 Paris
www.mnhn.fr
This is one of my favorite places to visit in Paris, so old-fashioned as the
animals roam down the center of the room in their skeletal form.

OST IN

USA

American Museum of Natural History
Central Park West at 79th Street
New York, NY 10024
www.amnh.org
I love this museum because every time you visit you discover something new.

Bell Museum of Natural History
Cnr. University Ave SE & 17th Ave
University of Minnesota, MN Campus
Minneapolis, MN 55455
www.bellmuseum.org

Getty Villa
17985 Pacific Coast Highway
Pacific Palisades, CA 90272
www.getty.edu/visit/

MAD
2 Columbus Circle
New York, NY 10019
www.madmuseum.org

The Mercer Museum
84 South Pine Street
Doylestown, PA 18901
www.mercermuseum.org
I discovered Fonthill, the passion and vision (some might say folly) of Henry C. Mercer, when I was on a *Gourmet* magazine shoot in Pennsylvania. The magical higgledy-piggledy concrete castle, lined with Moravian tiles he produced in his workshops, was built in the early 1900s to house his massive collection of everyday tools, hardware, machinery, finished products, and even an entire general store interior from the 1860s. Although I do not have the collecting bug for carts, canoes, and other larger scale objects, I did appreciate the impressive display of these things hanging and flying around the depths of the museum.

The Museum of Jurassic Technology
9341 Venice Boulevard
Culver City, CA 90232
www.mjt.org
Long ago I read *Mr. Wilson's Cabinet of Wonder*, which was based on an out-of-the-way place in LA, around way before Cabinets of Curiosities reached the resurgence of coolness they now enjoy. With limited time and the excuse of *Bowerbird*, I made an appointment to see the Museum of Jurassic Technology. Its unassuming façade, in a shade of green with an old brass buzzer engraved with its name, lovely and old school, was completely deceiving. I initially thought it was made up of just three rooms. In fact, two floors and a rabbit warren of roughly 20 rooms (I lost count so don't quote me on that) make up MJT. Each room is intimate, dark, and encourages you to look into, touch, listen, or read. It is a realization of one man's (& his wife's) vision.
Part carnevale, sideshow, history, circus, museum, & gallery – it's impossible to categorize. Each display is different, with dioramas, holograms, microscopes, 3D glasses, and listening devices for you to experience each strange and curious installation in its own way. Note to self: leave plenty of time – hours disappear here.

The Nutshell Studies of Unexplained Death
State of Maryland Medical Examiner's Office
111 Penn St
Baltimore, MD 21201

Shangri La
4055 Papu Circle
Honolulu, HI 96816
www.shangrilahawaii.org

Southern Vermont Natural History Museum
Route 9, Hogback Mountain
Marlboro, VT 05344
www.vermontmuseum.org

The Wagner Free Institute of Science of Philadelphia
1700 West Montgomery Ave
(Part of Public Library)
Philadelphia, PA 19121
www.wagnerfreeinstitute.org

AUSTRALIA

Bass Strait Shell Museum
12 Noel St
Apollo Bay, VIC 3233
www.cv.vic.gov.au/organisations/2882/bass-strait-shell-museum/
Shell collectors are a passionate lot as this is not the only museum housed in somebody's front room.

Bellview Shell Museum
10291 Bussell Highway
Witchcliffe, WA 6286
Super cool. This museum also lives in the front room of someone's house. There is crazy carpet on the floor and it offers some interesting decorative touches alongside the scientific collections.

Caroline Simpson Library
The Mint, 10 Macquarie Street
Sydney, NSW 2000
www.hht.net.au/research/library
The collection, which contains such things as journals, guides, wallpaper, and fabric, seems so personal: a real importance is placed on the hand touched, the individual – handwritten notes in a margin or personal references are embraced.
For *Bowerbird* research I spent an afternoon here poring over women's works: pressed fern albums, scrapbooks, and handmade albums containing cursive handwritten poems, sketches, portraits, watercolor flowers, pressed flowers, and other musings. The fern book photographed among these pages is housed at this resourceful library where I enjoy the treasures that unfold with the help of librarians Matthew and Michael.

Herbarium
The Royal Botanic Gardens
Sydney, NSW 2000
www.rbgsyd.nsw.gov.au
I always used to wonder why the NSW Herbarium is affectionately known as the Red Box, and have discovered that its name derives from the red boxes housing the mounted specimens, stacked so neatly in racks and piled high. The treasures within include a signed first edition copy of Darwin's *On the Origin of Species*, plus photographs and specimens found and mounted, on Cook's voyage, by Banks and Solander.
I have long wanted to get into the vaults and back-of-house, and managed to do so for *Bowerbird*. I was keen to see the specimens bottled in alcohol, but mostly I like the packaging: the old paper labels stuck on the front of the vessels, handwritten and documenting the contents. The glass vessels range from two to fifteen inches in height with varying diameters, and many are footed with straight sides and a fitted glass lid. Others appear to be old pickling jars and some of the tiny ones are in flat-based test tube shapes with corks fixed in the tops. I am looking forward to my next visit, to look at the moss albums and photographs of the original Herbarium in the Botanical Gardens.

Macleay Museum
Gosper Lane off Science Road
The University Of Sydney Campus
Sydney 2006
http://sydney.edu.au/museums/collections/macleay.shtml
I have frequented this gem for many years, greeted every time at the top of the stairs by a large pelican. The main room is lined with drawers and glass-fronted cabinets holding everything from mounted finches on turned posts to birdskins and pinned butterflies (the cards attached to the exhibits are often as interesting as the objects themselves). The museum houses the Macleay collection that once belonged to the well-known family of collectors of the same name, some of whom lived at Elizabeth Bay House in Sydney. For explorers, missionaries, & naturalists traveling in the Antipodes this was a must – an absolute treat.

Melbourne Museum
11 Nicholson St
Carlton, VIC 3053
www.museumvictoria.com.au/melbournemuseum
When I was horse riding recently, I stayed at the White family's Belltrees estate north of Sydney, and was fortunate enough to have a tour of the still-inhabited main house. In the corridor I noticed a handsome cabinet, which turned out to be for H. L. White's huge collection of Australian birdskins and eggs. The collection was bullocked down to Melbourne in the 1920s after a run-in with the Australian Museum in Sydney.
I flew to Melbourne to have a look and couldn't get over the beauty of the egg clusters; the huge variety of parrots, lyrebirds, bowerbirds, kingfishers, and pigeons; the birdskins, lying flat, stuffed with cotton wool and quietly stitched.
Each specimen is labeled – for consistency, White had labels made approximately four inches long and one inch wide, with room for details. I love the romance of the handwritten notes in ink, the different papers used for labels, as well as their shape & size.

Museum Of Old and New Art
655 Main Road
Berriedale, Tasmania 7011
mona.net.au
MONA is a very amusing curation, dictated and molded by its creator's desires and sense of humor. We need more eccentrics in the world! As artworks are unlabeled, you are supplied with an 'O' device on entry, which gives you descriptions, interviews, & ideas. The space is fitted out with honest materials and is full of old & new art. It is beautifully dark & ambient with a labyrinth of mezzanines and enclosed steel staircases, heightening your sense of curiosity. The journey, discovery, and sense of lost & found defines this space cut out of sandstone. There is no given or dictated path – it's choose your own adventure, so every time is different & unique!

INDIA

Alice Garg National Seashells Museum
10, Amit Bhardwaj Marg, Sector-7, Malviya Nagar
Jaipur-302 017, Rajasthan
www.aliceseashellmuseum.org

Amber Fort
Delhi-Jaipur Highway
11km from Jaipur, Rajasthan

The Calico Museum of Textiles
Sarabhai Foundation, opp. Underbridge,
Shahibag, Ahmedabad-380 004, Gujarat
www.calicomuseum.com

Mehrangarh Fort
Fort Rd
Jodhpur-342 006, Rajasthan
www.mehrangarh.org

The National Handicrafts and Handlooms Museum
Pragati Maidan, Bhairon Road
New Delhi
www.nationalcraftsmuseum.nic.in

National Museum
Maulana Azad Rd
New Delhi, Delhi
www.nationalmuseumindia.gov.in
This is all about the collection of Indian
miniature paintings.

CENTRAL ASIA

Karakalpak Museum of Arts
K. Rzaev Street
Nukus 230100 Karakalpakstan
Uzbekistan
www.savitskycollection.org

National Museum of Antiquities of Tajikistan
5 Academic Rajobov St
Dushanbe, Tajikistan

Sitora-i Mohi Khosa Summer Palace
Emir's Summer Palace
Two miles north of Bukhara
Uzbekistan
www.bukhara-museum.narod.ru

TURKEY

Istanbul Arkeoloji Müzeleri
Alemdar Cad. Osman Hamdi
Bey Yokuşu Sk, 34122
Sultanahmet/Fatih, Istanbul
www.istanbularkeoloji.gov.tr

ITALY

Palazzo Fortuny
San Marco 3958
30124 Venice
www.fortuny.visitmuve.it
Temporary exhibitions. I went to one curated
by Axel Vervoordt and it was mindblowing.

Villa San Michele
V.le Axel Munthe 34
80071 Anacapri
www.sanmichele.org

Museum of Natural History
University of Florence
Piazza di San Marco, 4
50121 Florence
www.msn.unifi.it

SHOPS&FLEA MARKETS I LOVE

USA

Alameda Point Antiques Faire
2900 Navy Way (at Main Street)
Alameda, CA 94501
www.alamedapointantiquesfaire.
com

Bell'occhio
10 Brady Street
San Francisco, CA 94103
www.bellocchio.com

The Bone Room
1569 Solano Ave
Berkeley, CA 94707
www.boneroom.com

The Evolution Store
120 Spring Street
New York, NY 10012
www.theevolutionstore.com

John Derian
6 & 10 East 2nd Street
New York, NY 10003
www.johnderian.com

Kiosk
95 Spring Street
New York, NY 10012
www.kioskkiosk.com

New York Central Art Supply
62 3rd Ave
New York, NY 10003
www.nycentralart.com

Obscura
207 Ave A
New York, NY 10009
www.obscuraantiques.com

Paula Rubenstein
65 Prince Street
New York, NY 10012

Paxton Gate
824 Valencia Street
(between 19th & 20th Streets)
San Francisco, CA 94110
www.paxtongate.com

Flax Art & Design
1699 Market St
San Francisco, CA 94103
www.flaxart.com

Second Hand Rose
230 5th Ave, Suite 510
Manhattan, NY 10010
www.secondhandrose.com

The Tail of the Yak
2632 Ashby Ave
Berkeley, CA 94705

Tinsel Trading
1 West 37th Street
New York, NY 10018
www.tinseltrading.com

PARIS

Au Bon Usage
21 rue Saint Paul
75004 Paris
www.aubonusage.com

Au Petit Fer à Cheval
30 rue Vieille du Temple
75004 Paris

BHV
52 rue de Rivoli
75189 Paris
www.bhv.fr
Just the hardware section.

Caravane
6 rue Pavée
75004 Paris
www.caravane.fr

Les Catacombes
1 Avenue du Colonel Henri Rol-
Tanguy
75014 Paris
www.catacombes-de-paris.fr
This is not a shop (unless you are
shopping for skulls).

Centre Pompidou Bookshop
Level 0, Centre Georges Pompidou
75004 Paris
www.cnac-gp.fr

Deyrolle
46 rue du Bac
75007 Paris
www.deyrolle.com

Hermès
24 rue du Faubourg Saint-Honoré
75008 Paris
www.hermes.com

Jambon & Brocante (Ham &
Antique Fair)
http://chatou.sncao-syndicat.com/
An annual market. Check website
for details.

Jamin Puech
68 rue Vieille du Temple
75003 Paris
www.jamin-puech.com

Marie Papier
26 rue Vavin
75006 Paris
www.mariepapier.fr

Merci
111 Boulevard Beaumarchais
75003 Paris

Muji
47 rue Francs Bourgeois
75004 Paris
www.muji.com

Objets de Notre Memoire
13 rue Saint Paul
75004 Paris

Porte de Vanves
Avenue Marc Sangnier & Avenue
Georges Lafenestre
75014 Paris

The Red Wheelbarrow
22 rue Saint Paul
75004 Paris
http://rwbooks.blogspot.com.au/

Tombées du Cambion
17 rue Joseph de Maistre
75018 Paris
This literally translates as "goods
fallen off the back of a truck."

AUSTRALIA

These are places of interest and the lovely shopowners who lent me their wares.

Anna-Wili Highfield
www.annawilihighfield.com
Anna-Wili makes ripped &
painted paper come to life by
sewing & sculpting it to create
creatures & critters.

Armadillo & Co
www.armadillo-co.com
Natural fiber rugs & dhurries in
perfectly simple patterns and
color combinations – a good
staple.

Bedouin Societe
www.bedouinsociete.com
This is just heaven. I only like
to sleep in linen and this has
the ultimate range – the perfect
weight & dyed colors. No frills.

Bonasera
www.bonasera.com.au
A modern version of a
wunderkammer – cast porcelain
bones and other curiosities.

Cadrys
498 Glenmore Rd
Edgecliff, NSW 2027
www.cadrys.com.au
Cadrys have every kind of a rug
you could ever be looking for –
from contemporary to vintage.

The Doll Hospital
38A Stoney Creek Rd
Bexley, NSW 2207
www.dollhospital.com.au

Jason Mowen Gallery
34 Redfern St
Redfern, NSW 2016
www.jasonmowen.com
Selection of original rugs from far-
fetched places plus key decorator
furniture pieces & art.

Julia deVille
www.juliadeville.com
See website for stockists.

Le Forge
59 Denison St
Camperdown, NSW 2050
www.leforge.com.au
A source for vintage French
salvage, lamps & chandeliers
galore, and new furniture based
on old designs. More warehouse
than shop.

Manon et Gwenaelle
Shop 2, 246 Palmer St
Darlinghurst, NSW 2010
Mostly French – all the things you
would want your kids to wear.

Megan Park
www.meganpark.co.uk
Cushions & throws embellished
with beads, sequins, & embroidery.
All of her fabrics and color
combinations are beautiful.

Mr Cook
318 New South Head Rd
Double Bay, NSW 2028
www.mrcook.com.au
Sean is more than a florist. He
has been going to the markets for
many years and always finds the
most perfect natural things I didn't
know I was looking for.

Noelle Rigaudie
crigaudie@bigpond.net.au
Recycled cardboard furniture,
chandeliers, & frames. Most
often painted in black or white.
Available for commission.

Object Gallery
417 Bourke St
Surry Hills, NSW 2010
www.object.com.au
Supporting Australian artists &
craftspeople.

Orson & Blake
483 Riley St
Surry Hills, NSW 2010
www.orsonandblake.com.au
Cool new furniture sourced from
around the globe, a bit mix &
match.

Seasonal Concepts
122 Redfern St
Redfern, NSW 2016
www.seasonalconcepts.com.au
Magic & fantasy curated by the
talented Ken Wallis. Furniture &
menagerie sourced with a keen eye.

Seneca
76A Paddington St
Paddington, NSW 2021
www.senecatextiles.com
Supplying fabric to the trade and
representing some of the greats
from Lorca to JAB, Osborne &
Little, amongst others.

The Society inc.
18 Stewart St
Paddington, NSW 2021
This is my shop & has everything
that you may need if you are into
haberdashery & hardware with a
big dose of curios.

Space
84 O'Riordan St
Alexandria, NSW 2015
www.spacefurniture.com.au
A mecca for big names in the
design world.

Strangetrader Byron Bay
Shop 4, Byron Arcade
13 Lawson St
Byron Bay, NSW 2481
www.strangetrader.com

Tara Badcock
www.paristasmania.com
A genius on the sewing machine,
patching vintage & new fabrics
while she embroiders, textures,
& rosettes to create one-off
pieces that appear as if they are
illustrated artworks.

Tarlo & Graham Melbourne
60 Chapel Street
Windsor, VIC 3181
www.tarloandgraham.com

BOOKS I REFERENCE

1000 Degrees Celsius Deyrolle by Laurent Bochet

Amulets: Sacred Charms of Power and Protection by Sheila Paine

The Antique & Flea Markets of Italy by Marina Seveso

The Ashley Book of Knots by Clifford W. Ashley

Atlas of Remote Islands by Judith Schalansky

Birds of Paradise and Bower Birds by William T. Cooper and Joseph M. Forshaw

Blackstock's Collections: The Drawings of an Artistic Savant by Gregory L. Blackstock

The Book of Answers by Carol Bolt

Botanical Riches: Stories of Botanical Exploration by Richard Aitken

Butterflies of New Zealand by W. B. R. Laidlaw

Cabinet of Natural Curiosities by Albertus Seba

Canoe Country & Snowshoe Country by Florence Page Jaques, Justine Kerfoot and Francis Lee Jaques

Cicero: The Life and Times of Rome's Greatest Politician by Anthony Everitt

The Coney Island Amateur Psychoanalytic Society and Its Circle by Aaron Beebe, Zoe Beloff, Amy Herzog and Norman Klein

Cook's Pacific Encounters by National Museum of Australia

The Coral Thief by Rebecca Stott

Darwin and the Barnacle: The Story of One Tiny Creature and History's Most Spectacular Scientific Breakthrough by Rebecca Stott

Doris Duke's Shangri La by Sharon Littlefield

An Edwardian Summer: Sydney and Beyond Through the Lens of Arthur Wigram Allen by Judith Ainge, Alan Davies and Howard Tanner

French General: Treasured Notions by Kaari Meng

Heath Ceramics by Amos Klausner

Herbarium by Robyn Stacey and Ashley Hay

How to be an Explorer of the World by Keri Smith

I Married Adventure: The Lives of Martin and Osa Johnson by Osa Johnson

Jamrach's Menagerie by Carol Birch

Japanese Country Textiles by Anna Jackson

Just My Type: A book about Fonts by Simon Garfield

Karl Blossfeldt: The Complete Published Work by Hans-Christian Adam and Karl Blossfeldt

Linnaeus: The Compleat Naturalist by Wilfrid Blunt

The Love India Guides by Fiona Caulfield

The Lunar Men: Five Friends Whose Curiosity Changed the World by Jenny Uglow

All books by Mark Dion

Thank you

My very capable & amazing assistants Leah and Hannah, Leta Keens,
my dad, Donna Hay, Edwina McCann, James Merrell,
Matilda Duffecy, my sister Nicole, Anna & Pete Schutzinger, and my
brother/photographer, Chris Court.

Daisy, Polly, & Fox for being very good models.

For the lovely locations I was kindly loaned:
Mickey of Glenmore House
Justin & Bettina Hemmes
Sally Campbell & Greg Stitt
Collette Dinnigan & Bradley Cocks
Carriageworks
The Bite Club
Annie Schutzinger

A goodbye to Peppergreen, a collector's haven & resource for 20 years.

Museum of Victoria
Macleay Museum, & curator, Jude Philp
Caroline Simpson Library, librarians Michael & Matthew
Historic Houses Trust
Herbarium, Dale Dixon

To all the assistants who helped out on photoshoots.

ec amour

HarperCollins books may be purchased for educational, business, or sales promotional
use. For information, please write: Special Markets Department, HarperCollins*Publishers*,
10 East 53rd Street, New York, NY 10022.

First published in Australia in 2012
by HarperCollins*Publishers* Australia Pty Limited

First published in the USA in 2012 by:
Harper Design,
An Imprint of HarperCollins*Publishers*
10 East 53rd Street
New York, NY 10022
Tel: (212) 207–7000
Fax: (212) 207–7654
harperdesign@harpercollins.com
www.harpercollins.com

ISBN: 978-0-06223685-2
Library of Congress Control Number: 2012940697

Styling and concept: Sibella Court
Art direction and design: Hannah Brady and Sibella Court
Editors: Leah Rauch and Leta Keens
Colour reproduction by Graphic Print Group, South Australia

Printed and bound in China by RR Donnelley
First printing, 2012